MODERN DRUMMER® Presents:

FUNdamentals™ of Drumming for Kids

Percussion theory for children ages 5 to 10

Developed by Rich Redmond and Michael Aubrecht

Visit us online at
moderndrummer.com/fundamentalsofdrumming

Subscribe to *Modern Drummer*, the world's best drumming magazine,
at moderndummer.com/subscribe

For more fun and educational videos, subscribe to the
"Modern Drummer Official" YouTu...

Modern Drummer Publisher/CEO Davic

Modern Drummer Worldwide Education Dom Famularo

Edited by Michael Dawson

Layout by Scott Bienstock

Front cover photo by Paul Griffin

Back cover photo by William Mahone

Published by:
Modern Drummer Publications, Inc.
315 Ridgedale Ave #478
East Hanover, NJ 07936

I have fond memories of the first time that I actually saw a drum. My parents, Rita and Silviano Frangioni, got me a toy drum, randomly at first. It had paper drumheads, so as soon as I started bashing on it the heads broke! However, that was enough to fuel the drummer inside of me, and I was hooked. I was eighteen months old. Soon after, I was diagnosed with retinoblastoma (cancer of the eye), and the trauma of having my right eye removed and a prosthetic implanted was daunting. The drums were a refuge. They became my joy, my passion, and my creative outlet, and that stands true to this day. I once heard that "you don't find the drums; the drums find you," meaning that all drummers have a deep passion for the instrument that's indescribable. Today, I am blessed to publish the #1 resource in the world dedicated to fueling drummers with exclusive insight, education, and inspiration—a perpetual acclamation of drums, drummers, and drumming! *Modern Drummer*'s educational tools inspire and instruct players at all levels and styles, and it unbelievably rewarding to do so, especially for children. I hope you have as much fun learning from this book as we did creating it. Once you've gone through it, check out the many other titles available in *Modern Drummer*'s ever-growing library of drum books and publications. Stay inspired!

David Frangioni
CEO/Publisher Modern Drummer Publications, Inc.

Welcome to learning the drumset! This will be an exciting journey. *FUNdamentals of Drumming for Kids* will be your tour guide to the joy and understanding of drumming. Co-author Rich Redmond is a top player, educator, and communicator, and he brings *fun* into practicing. He will take you through a step-by-step process of learning basic technique to moving around the drumset. Follow along with Rich in the supplemental videos as you explore the world of drumset fundamentals. You are the next generation of musicians. Find your own beat, and then share it. Onward and upward!

Dom Famularo
"Drumming's Global Ambassador"
Modern Drummer Worldwide Education

This book is dedicated to the next generation of drum heroes.

*Pictured: Rich's 2012 DW Collector's Series Maple/Mahogany drumkit (Photo: Paul Griffin)

CONTENTS

From the Professional 4

From the Parent 5

Introduction 6

History of Drums.. 8

Evolution of the Drumset 9

Famous Drummers 11

Famous Kid Drummers.. 14

Types of Drums 15

Parts of the Drumset 16

Drumstick Dexterity 18

Note Recognition 19

Counting.. 28

Stretches and Warm-Ups 32

FUNdamentals Program 34

Clapping Exercises 35

Tapping Exercises 36

Hand Drumming.. 37

Note Groupings... 38

Introduction to Rudiments 39

Pattern Phrases... 40

The Dynamic Duo.. 41

Foot Focus... 42

The Money Beats 46

Alone and Together... 47

Recommendations.. 48

Foot Exercises 49

Three-Way Independence... 53

Four-Way Independence 61

Fun With Toms!.. 69

16th Notes... 74

Pea Soup: Mmm-Mmm Good!... 82

Going Global: World Beats 88

Your First Drum Solo!.. 90

Tips and Tricks... 91

Fun and Games 92

Parting Philosophy.. 94

Acknowledgements 95

FROM THE PROFESSIONAL

I love rhythm. As a drummer, it means everything to me.

Rhythm is the primary source of my inspiration and the driving force behind my self-expression. Sharing my love of rhythm is what this book is all about. In fact, the primary purpose behind the *FUNdamentals of Drumming for Kids* program is to help children discover the same love for rhythm that I have. As a professional musician and educator, I always knew there was a way to break the ice on this subject and to systematically introduce young students to the language of music making.

This book was inspired by a conversation with my friend Michael Aubrecht. While many readers may be familiar with Michael's work as an author and film producer, they may be surprised to know that he is also a drummer. In fact, Michael and I are both products of music education, and we share many of the same drumming influences. As a parent, Michael was seeking guidance on the best way to introduce his youngest son to the drums. After doing some research, we both concluded that there were few materials available that catered to very young drummers. It was then that the *FUNdamentals* system was born. By pairing proven drum teaching methods with elementary classroom exercises, we developed a new teaching philosophy.

The *FUNdamentals of Drumming for Kids* program uses a step-by-step process in which each exercise builds upon the previous one. Although being a drummer certainly helps, the lessons in this book are designed in such a way that non-drumming parents can also practice them alongside their children. The book is also set up in a format that can be easily adapted by general classroom music teachers. The core of the *FUNdamentals* philosophy is found in the kid-friendly techniques that are used to present music theory.

As an extension of the book, we have developed moderndrummer.com/fundamentalsofdrumming, where additional drumming activities and exercises have been made available. We encourage parents and teachers to share their own success stories by emailing photos, videos, and stories of them using *FUNdamentals of Drumming for Kids*. Selections from those submitted will be posted and shared with our online community.

Michael and I sincerely hope that you enjoy using this book as much as we enjoyed writing it. Visit me online at richredmond.com. Here's to the rhythm of life!

Rich Redmond

FROM THE PARENT

Long before I was anything else, I was a drummer. In fact, it wouldn't be an exaggeration to say that for most of my adolescent life, drums meant everything to me. Following the path of many eager musicians, I took up the instrument in the seventh grade and quickly became the prototypical band kid, playing in the choir band, marching band, stage band, symphonic band, and percussion ensemble.

A product of public school music education, I practiced hard and was designated the co-captain of my high school drum line. I was selected to participate in the Pitt University High School Senior Ensemble and the Mellon Jazz Festival Student Orchestra. I played at the national level in marching band and drum line competitions in Nashville and was fortunate to study with some great percussionists. I also jammed with anybody and everybody who would have me.

As a father of four, I was very excited to see my son Jackson (pictured above) beginning to show an interest in the drums. Unfortunately, I was also very disappointed in the lack of instructional aids available for children under the age of ten. Out of frustration, I decided to contact Rich Redmond, who is one of the most respected drummers in the music business. Rich's reputation as a top clinician and teacher precedes him, and my goal was to ask for his guidance and share the successes I had experienced, using simple counting and playing exercises at home.

Somehow I managed to catch Rich's attention long enough to pitch the need for instructional drum lessons geared toward children. Knowing that I was a writer who played the drums, Rich suggested that we tackle this dilemma together. A few weeks later, we found ourselves sitting together backstage at a Jason Aldean show, drafting an outline that evolved into the system we refer to as *FUNdamentals*. Today, we are great friends, and we are developing an entire drum education program together.

As a parent, I can tell you that this program will provide enjoyment for kids of all ages and stages of development. Rich and I simply want to see kids experiencing the joys of drumming, no matter what goals they attain or what skill levels they achieve. Visit me online at pinstripepress.net. Play on!

Michael Aubrecht

INTRODUCTION

The auditory stimulation of sound is one of the first sensations experienced by humans. Many experts believe that music, in particular, offers a welcome sense of security to the unborn child. As they grow, children continue to rely on music as an important element in the learning experience. This is why parents and teachers rely on the repetition of a song as a teaching aid. Music promotes memory!

Many parts of a child's first skill set come from singing exercises, such as the ABC song. These repetitive patterns enable children to subconsciously correlate the cadence of the music to the material, thus helping them to remember it. Music is, therefore, a major brick in a child's foundation of learning.

Children at the early-developmental stage can be extremely creative and far less inhibited than those who are older. Often they will develop a desire to make their own sounds. Some may even show an interest in playing music. This can be a wonderfully exciting time. Parents may wish to seize this opportunity to introduce their child to a variety of musical styles and instruments. Sometimes the child will gravitate toward a particular instrument, and he or she may even show an aptitude for it. It is at this stage that a teaching opportunity exists. If handled correctly, it may even result in the pursuit of mastery of that musical instrument.

Drums can be an excellent choice for a young child's first instrument. Whether it's banging on pots and pans or pounding away on a tom, playing percussion is a great release of energy. Playing the drumkit can also be an excellent way to exercise and develop manual dexterity. Sometimes a child will start out with a toy drum, a practice pad, or a simple snare drum before graduating to a real drumkit. Regardless of the instrument, the fundamentals of drumming remain the same.

How to Use This Book

This book has been written so it can be used by individual children (ages 5–10) and by multiple students in a classroom. Parents and teachers are strongly encouraged to read aloud to guide younger students. Older children should be able to read and comprehend the material on their own. This book is complemented with exclusive videos shot at Drum Channel Studios. In the videos, you'll find additional information and playing examples of the FUNdamentals philosophy and exercises in this book.

The videos are available via the "FUNdamentals of Drumming for Kids" playlist on the Modern Drummer Official YouTube channel.

Program Overview

FUNdamentals of Drumming for Kids is exactly what it sounds like: a fun way of introducing the basics of drumming to children who are between the ages of 5 and 10. Although there have been many programs developed for teaching music theory to children, few cater to younger age groups. This has resulted in a lack of educational techniques and lesson plans for kids.

That is…until now.

The unique approach used in this book to teach young children the basics of percussion utilizes a combination of rudimentary rhythmic lessons and basic drumming exercises. By using a combination of enjoyable and familiar learning techniques, children are able to gain a better understanding of rhythm and the basic philosophies of playing drums. Each step in this program is designed to develop practical and applicable musical skills.

FUNdamentals

Most introductory drum lessons for children involve reading and a series of rigid rudimentary exercises that are repeated over and over in a monotonous fashion. This repetitive process ultimately results in muscle memory and can work well with older children, but it is not likely to captivate and hold the attention of younger students. Many of them lose interest due to an inability to establish a relationship between the exercises and making music. They are unable to comprehend the end result, because the material is not presented in an appropriate manner for their age group. More often than not, this inability to make that crucial connection results in the child abandoning the instrument before he or she even has a chance to get started.

The *FUNdamentals of Drumming for Kids* program uses a variety of teaching techniques that mimic a curriculum taught in an elementary classroom. These exercises present drum theory in a fun and familiar way by using flash cards, counting exercises, clapping, shape recognition, sound interpretation, motion mimicking, and more. You may notice that we have also **highlighted** important words, numbers, and phrases throughout the book to help introduce students to the vocabulary of drumming.

FUNdamentals of Drumming for Kids = Age-Appropriate Music Theory

Note: This book is not just a music manual. It is an activity book full of breathing room and space. Children should be encouraged to use it like a workbook by taking notes, doodling, and creating their own fun while the program progresses. When they complete the book, they will have a diary of FUNdamentals that they can look back on and be proud of.

HISTORY OF DRUMS

The drum is a member of the percussion family of instruments. It creates sound by being struck with some type of object, like a rounded stick, and the playing surface is often some type of stretched skin. Drums are the world's oldest instruments and have remained relatively the same for thousands of years.

The first drumming was done by clapping or by slapping hands on the chest and thighs. The first musical rhythms were performed using these methods. Instruments were later created so that drummers could play louder.

The first drums were made from hollowed-out logs covered in animal skins. They were played by hand or with a drumstick or mallet. These drums were used to communicate and entertain. Early cultures played drums to celebrate victory in battle and during ritual dances. Tribes played drums to share messages between villages. You might say that the drum was the world's first cell phone!

Drums were also used by armies to give commands during war. Roman legion drummers played pounding rhythms, called cadences, that told the soldiers what to do and where to go. During the American Civil War, drummer boys would march with the soldiers, playing a special parade beat to help keep them in step.

At the beginning of the twentieth century, people began putting different kinds of drums together. This formed the drumkit, which was also called the **trapset**. It is a group of percussion instruments that are set up to be played by one person. The basic drumset includes a **bass drum**, a **snare drum**, **tom-toms**, a **hi-hat**, and **cymbals**.

The earliest drummers were tasked with keeping time for the other musicians. As music evolved, so did the drummer's job. In time, drum rolls and fills became integral parts of songs. In the 1930s, drummers used small drumkits for playing jazz and ragtime music. In the 1940s, drummers started using larger drumsets to **swing** in big band orchestras. The best players of this era included Chick Webb, Jo Jones, Gene Krupa, and Buddy Rich.

Over the years, different kinds of music have changed the drumset and how it is played. In the 1960s, rock 'n' roll drummers often played long solos. In the 1970s, drummers began to show off at concerts by placing their drumsets on raised platforms, lifting them high in the air. Electronic drums and drum machines came along in the 1980s, and computer-based drum software followed in the 1990s.

Today there are many different kinds of drummers. But no matter what type of drumkit or music they play, they all have the same job: to keep the beat!

EVOLUTION OF THE DRUMSET

19th Century

The origins of the modern drumset can be traced all the way back to the mid-nineteenth century, when African-American slaves began using different-size drums to play along with spiritual music. These instruments were handmade and based on the drums that were used to communicate between villages back in their homeland. The design of the drums was quite remarkable, and many percussionists today use similar types of drums, like modern congas and bongos.

The first formal drumset originated when drummers decided to combine different percussion instruments together into a single **set** or **kit**. During the late nineteenth century, brass bands were very popular. Most cities in America had a bandstand in the center of town where concerts were held on the weekends. Many of these bands were formed by military men, while others were made up of local musicians. All of them marched or played to the beat of drummers. Most of the bands contained two or more drummers that each played a snare, a bass drum, or cymbals.

The concept of one drummer playing two or more parts was made possible only through the invention of the snare drum stand and bass drum pedal. These new products meant that drummers no longer had to carry their instruments. It also meant that a single drummer could play more than one drum at a time.

The first drumset was called a **contraption** and included a variety of percussion instruments, including a bass drum, a snare, toms, sandpaper blocks, gongs, woodblocks, triangles, cowbells, and a bent cymbal stand called a **gooseneck**.

1920s

By the 1920s the contraption setup became the standard for drummers to play. This period also saw the invention of the **low boy**, which was the first version of what we now call the **hi-hat**. This invention allowed drummers to clap two small cymbals together by pushing down on a pedal with their foot. The low boy was then modified to bring the cymbals up higher, so that swing drummers, like Jo Jones with the Count Basie Orchestra, could use them to play time with their hands. This became known as the **sock cymbal**. Drummers in the Roaring Twenties also began using fly swatters and brushes to play their drums more quietly to create new sounds.

1930s

As popular music continued to expand, so did the drumset. Big bands became the trendy groups of the day, and the need for a much bigger, stronger, and faster drum sound came about. One of the most talented and popular drummers of this period was Gene Krupa. In addition to playing some of the best solos in big band music, he also helped to develop the modern version of the jazz drumset. Krupa added a larger bass drum and used mounted toms and multiple floor toms. He also incorporated many cymbals of different types and sizes. These would later evolve into the ride, crash, and splash cymbals that we use today. Some drummers during this era went even further than Krupa by adding two bass drums and timpani to their kits.

1940s

In New York City throughout the 1940s, small groups of musicians began playing a new kind of music that was meant more for listening than dancing. Drummers were no longer used simply as timekeepers, and many began playing more complex parts. These jazzy drummers were called bebop players, and their style of club drumming called for smaller drumsets. The music also required a different level of sound, as the drums no longer had to project beyond a bandstand full of musicians to the back of a hopping dance hall.

1950s

New kinds of drum shells were developed in the 1950s that allowed for better tuning control, and plastic drumheads soon followed. Until this time, drumheads had been made from animal skins. The heads were hard to maintain and often changed in pitch and tone according to the weather. In the mid-'50s, the first synthetic (plastic) drumhead was introduced. The '50s also saw new developments and improvements in cymbal stands and hardware, as well as in drumstick designs.

1960s

By the late 1960s, popular music had become quite a bit louder, which brought back the need for a larger drumset. Rock musicians often embraced a **double bass** setup, and many began adding more cymbals and mounted toms. Drum solos also became popular again, just as they had been during the big band era. Most drums during this period were manufactured to be thicker, larger, and stronger in order to withstand the heavy hitting that had become the norm.

1970s

In the 1970s, single-headed concert toms became very popular and were used for live performances as well as in the recording studio. The idea behind concert toms was that because of the absence of the bottom heads, the drums would project more. Some companies also began experimenting with drums crafted from different materials. John Bonham of Led Zeppelin played on a see-through acrylic drumset. More durable, heavyweight cymbal stands and tom holders were also developed in the '70s.

1980s and 1990s

The 1980s saw a variety of innovations for the drumset. Heavy metal drummers began assembling huge drumsets that sometimes wrapped all the way around them. These monster kits were often customized with special sizes and exciting paint schemes. Electronic drums and sequencers were introduced during this era as well. These drums were made up of flat rubber pads that were attached to a computer, allowing the drummer to play hundreds of sounds from just a single pad. Things changed in the 1990s, as many drummers began going back to smaller acoustic drumkits. This simpler style of four- and five-piece drumsets has remained popular among many of today's players.

2000s to Today

As we entered the twenty-first century, drummers had more choices in setups and equipment than ever before. Drum, cymbal, and percussion manufacturers began to offer custom designs that enabled players to order a personalized drumkit that was tailored to their needs. Junior drumsets were also introduced to the market so that younger children could learn to play on an instrument that was just like an adult's setup, only smaller. Innovations in computer software and digital recording equipment enabled drummers to sound better, and popular music-based video games, like *Rock Band*, allowed non-musicians to play along to their favorite music without the need for an actual drumset. Today, drummers often incorporate elements from both the past and the present.

Stay tuned to see what the future holds!

FAMOUS DRUMMERS (1920s–1950s)

Chick Webb

Baby Dodds

Gene Krupa

Buddy Rich

Jo Jones

Max Roach

Cozy Cole

Shelly Manne

Sandy Nelson

FAMOUS DRUMMERS (1950s–1980s)

DJ Fontana

Earl Palmer

Ringo Starr

Keith Moon

Ginger Baker

John Bonham

Steve Gadd

Steve Smith

Neil Peart

FAMOUS DRUMMERS (1980s–Today)

Alex Van Halen

Stewart Copeland

Sheila E

Dave Grohl

Carter Beauford

Travis Barker

Ahmir "Questlove" Thompson

Mike Portnoy

Terry Bozzio

FAMOUS KID DRUMMERS

Buddy Rich is considered by many to be one of the greatest musicians of all time. He was an American drummer and bandleader who began his music career as a child. Buddy's talent for playing rhythm was first noted by his father, who saw that he could keep a steady beat with spoons at the age of one. Buddy began playing the drums in vaudeville when he was eighteen months old and was billed as "Traps, the Drum Wonder." At the peak of his childhood career, Buddy was reportedly the second-highest-paid child entertainer in the world. At eleven, he was already working as a bandleader. Buddy's versatile playing style and his ability to play lightning-fast

rolls enabled him to play in many different bands with many different musicians. He performed jazz, swing, big band, and bebop. Buddy continued to play drums for the rest of his life and is still admired for his incredible technique and speed.

> **"I think that any young drummer starting out today should get himself a great teacher and learn all there is to know about the instrument that he wants to play." —Buddy Rich**

Often referred to as a "percussion prodigy," **Tony Royster Jr.** has participated in numerous drum contests, including the 1995 Guitar Center Drum-Off national competition, which he won at the age of eleven. (Co-author Rich Redmond competed against Tony in this battle.) Tony was also voted the top up-and-coming drummer by *Modern Drummer* magazine in 2000. He appeared on the cover of the millennium issue of *Modern Drummer* and continues to receive praise. Tony has performed alongside such notable drummers as Dennis Chambers, Billy Cobham, Steve Smith, Sheila E, and Chester Thompson, and he has toured with top acts, including hip-hop mogul Jay-Z.

> **"My favorite part of being a drummer is watching people dance and enjoy themselves while I'm playing. It keeps me motivated to continue doing what I love to do: make music." —Tony Royster Jr.**

Buddy Rich and Tony Royster Jr. are just two examples that prove that even kids can become great drummers if they take the time to practice their instrument and, most important, have fun!

TYPES OF DRUMS

Encourage the child to color these images for increased retention.

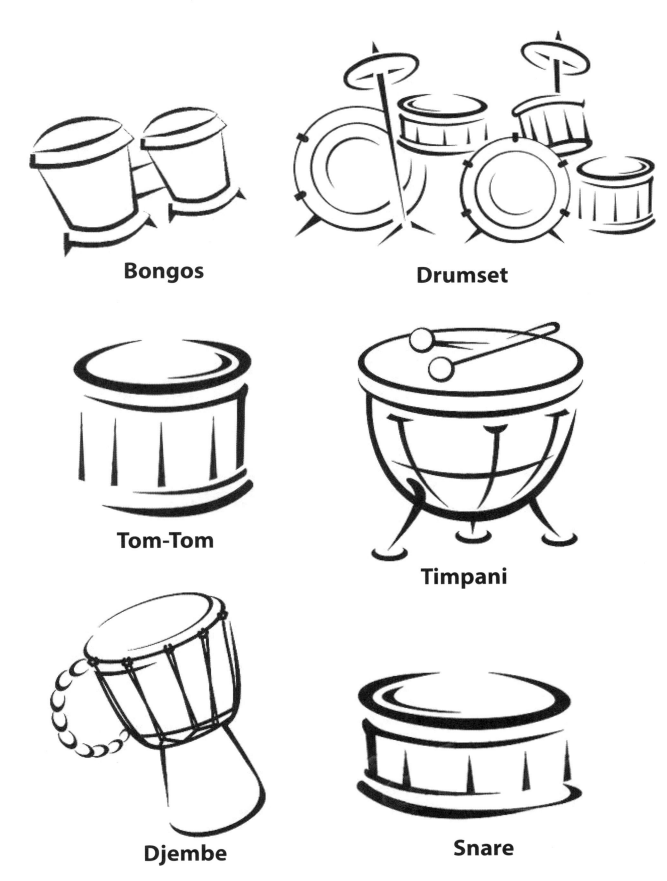

Bongos

Drumset

Tom-Tom

Timpani

Djembe

Snare

PARTS OF THE DRUMSET

Crash or Ride Cymbal

(Mounted) Rack Toms

Hi-Hat

Floor Tom

Snare

Bass Drum

The drumset is made up mostly of a series of objects shaped like circles and cylinders. Each drum and cymbal can be a different size and make a different sound. (The smaller the drum, the higher the sound. The larger the drum, the lower the sound.) Drummers tighten and loosen the drumheads on the shells in order to get different tones. This process is called **tuning**. Drummers can use sticks, mallets, and brushes to produce many different sounds. Some drummers use a big drumset with two bass drums and a lot of toms and cymbals, while others opt for a much smaller drumset.

Count how many drums and cymbals there are on your drumset. Use the following page like a coloring book to help you remember the names of the different parts. Then visit moderndrummer.com/ fundamentalsofdrumming to download and print a version to cut out and label the parts of your kit.

BASS

RIDE

SNARE

HI-HAT

TOM

CRASH

TOM

CRASH

FLOOR TOM

DRUMSTICK DEXTERITY

Many drummers today hold their drumsticks using the **matched grip** technique. The matched grip involves gripping the sticks with the index and middle fingers and curling them around the bottom of the stick, with the thumb resting on the side. The base of the stick sits in the center of the palm, with the end of the stick resting comfortably in the hand.

Matched grip is essentially an extension of the arm that creates a fulcrum to allow the stick to move freely and bounce after striking the drum. The index finger and thumb are used to hold the stick, while the bottom three fingers are used to propel the stick.

Matched Grip Basics

1. Find a point on the stick about one-third of the way up from the bottom end. Grab the stick between the thumb and the spot between the first and second knuckles of the index finger. Wrap your fingers loosely around the drumstick. Each of the back three fingers should touch the stick. Don't squeeze it; hold it loosely.

2. With the palms of your hands facing down, make a triangle shape with the drumsticks by putting the two tips together. This creates the **Power V** position. You are now ready to play!

3. When preparing to hit the drum, make sure your shoulders and elbows are relaxed. Keep a firm but relaxed grip on the stick with all fingers. The tips of the drumsticks should meet in the center of the drum.

4. You might want to take a small, circular object (like a soda can) and trace it in the middle of the drumhead. This will act as a target and will remind you to use the proper grip in order to hit the drum in the same place each time.

*Note: Although the matched grip is considered to be more popular among modern drumset players, the **traditional grip** is an alternative technique that was originally devised for marching drummers, who carried their drums at a slant on a shoulder sling. Both authors favor matched grip, as it is more symmetrical and can be used universally across the entire spectrum of percussion instruments.*

NOTE RECOGNITION

This section provides a basic introduction to reading percussion music. The ability to understand it in its entirety will depend on the child's age and comprehension level.

Why is it important to read music?

All musicians, no matter what instrument they play, should have a basic understanding of reading music. Every form of music with a beat needs a drummer, and drummers who can read and write music are far better prepared to play than those who cannot. From classical compositions to heavy metal riffs and everything in between, musical notation is the road map of a song. Without it, you might get lost. Musicians have their very own ABCs for reading and writing music. Drum ABCs are made up of shapes and symbols called **notations**. All music is written on five long lines called a **staff**. With drums, these notes are written on different spaces and lines that represent different parts of the drumset. This tells the drummer what to hit and when to hit it. The drummer's alphabet is made up of circles, ovals, triangles, and X's.

Drum Notation

| Crash | Hi-Hat | Ride | Ride Bell | Tom 1 | Snare | Tom 2 | Bass Drum |

Time Signatures

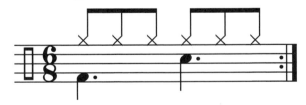

Drummers are also called **timekeepers** because they tell the rest of the band how fast or slow to play. Drummers use notations called **time signatures** to guide them on how to subdivide the basic pulse of the song. These are written at the beginning of a piece of music.

The top number tells you how many counts there are before you repeat. (Each repeat is called a **measure**.) The bottom number gives the length of each count. In 3/4 time, there are three counts in the measure, and the quarter note gets one count. In 6/8 time (example above), there are six counts in the measure, and the 8th note gets one count.

Pyramid of Notes

These are the five most basic note types, starting from the four-count whole note and then subdividing it in half four times until you reach 16th notes, which are called that because there are sixteen of them in each measure of music that's in a 4/4 time signature.

Whole Note

Half Notes

Quarter Notes

8th Notes

16th Notes

Now that we've learned about time signatures and notes, let's learn how to notate when *not* to play.

Pyramid of Rests

Just as notes tell the drummer when to play a beat, rests tell the drummer when *not* to play . A **rest** is an interval (or count) of silence in a piece of music, marked by a symbol that indicates the length of the pause. Each rest symbol corresponds with a particular note value. In musical patterns, the notes we don't hear (rests) are just as important as the notes we do hear. Both are needed in order to establish a rhythm and break the repetition of steady beats. Even though they are silent, rests have the same duration (or time value) as their matching notes.

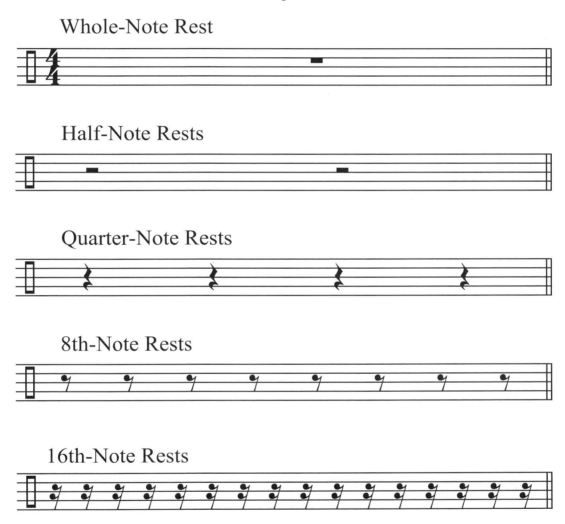

Whole-Note Rest

Half-Note Rests

Quarter-Note Rests

8th-Note Rests

16th-Note Rests

Drummers have to keep counting every beat, even when they're not playing. This means they must include the notes and the rests in their counts. A pattern that goes **beat – beat – beat – rest** is still counted as **1 – 2 – 3 – 4**, with the first three counts representing a stroke and the last count representing silence.

Try coming up with some counting patterns that mix beats and rests. Clap or snap along as you count each beat, and remember to *skip* the snap or clap on each rest (but be sure to count it). Start out simple, and then try creating more complex combinations.

Now that we've learned about time signatures, notes, and rests, let's "eat"!

Notation Nutrition: Let's Make a Percussion Pizza!

Another way to look at the difference between music notes is to think of them as different-size slices of pizza. A whole note would be a pizza that has yet to be sliced. Half notes would be the two parts of a pizza that has been cut in half. Quarter notes equal four cuts of pizza (or four quarters), 8th notes are eight cuts, and 16th notes equal sixteen slices.

Download the following puzzle pieces from moderndrummer.com/fundamentalsofdrumming, cut them out, and place them over the pizza-pan template on the previous page. See how each note makes up an equal portion of our percussion pizza. (Are you getting hungry?)

Whole Note

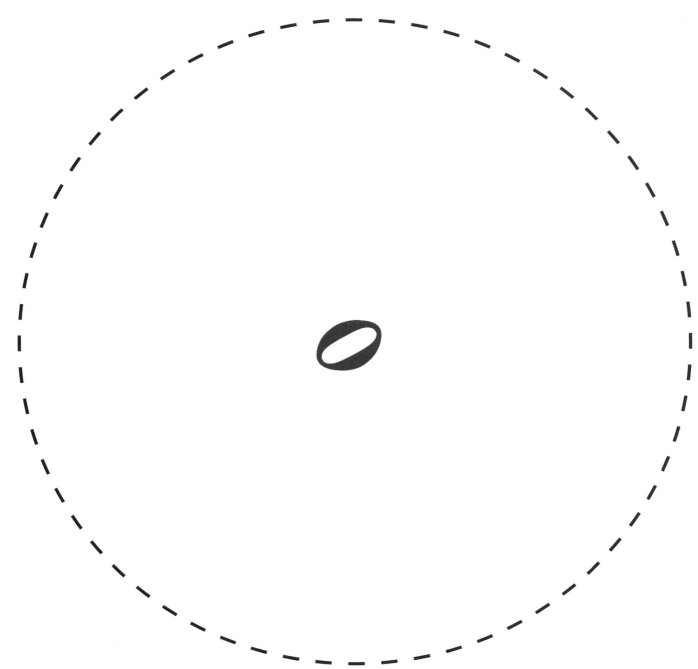

Half Notes

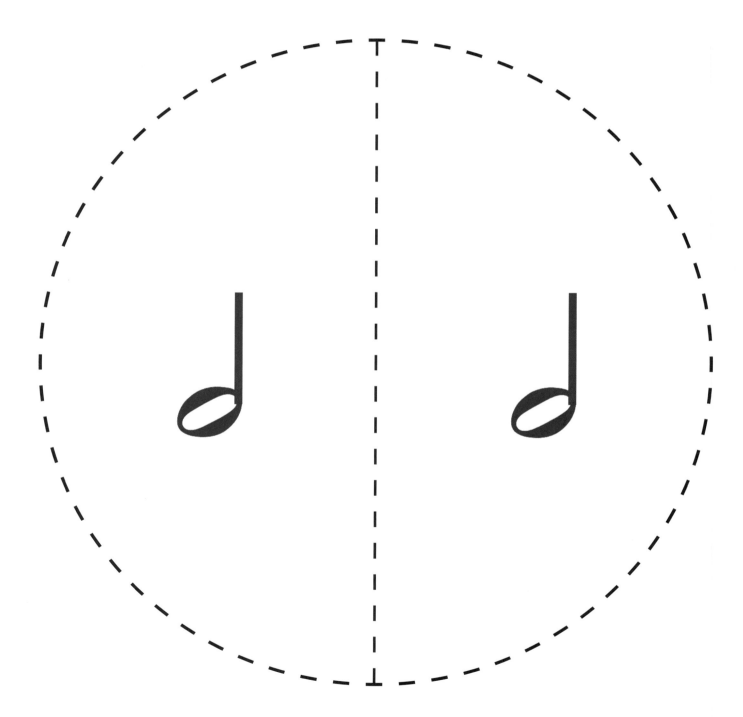

Quarter Notes

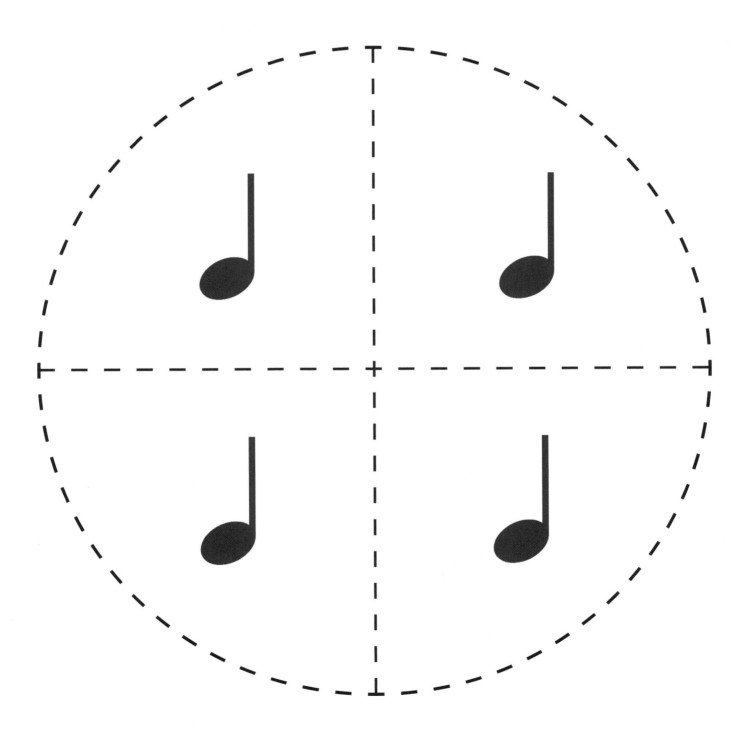

8th Notes

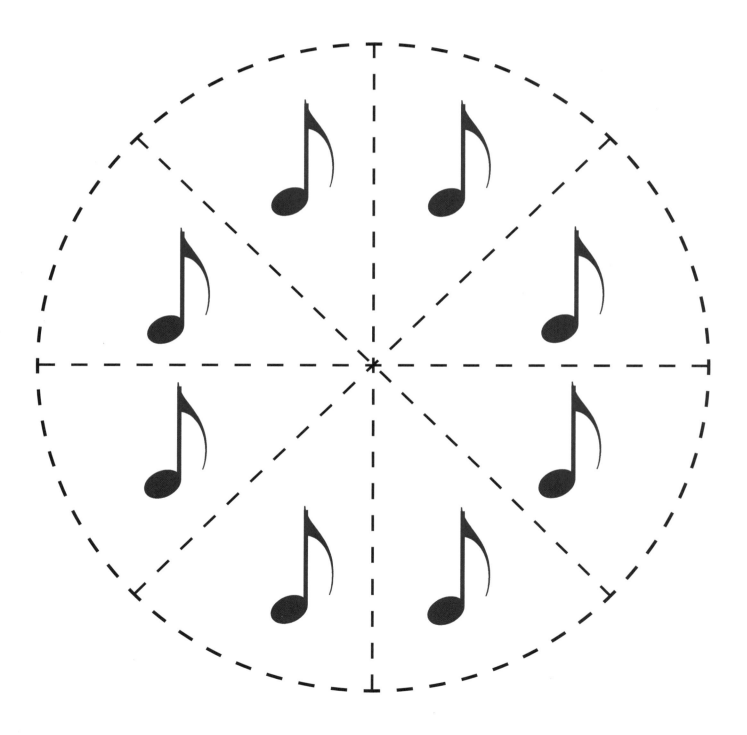

16th Notes

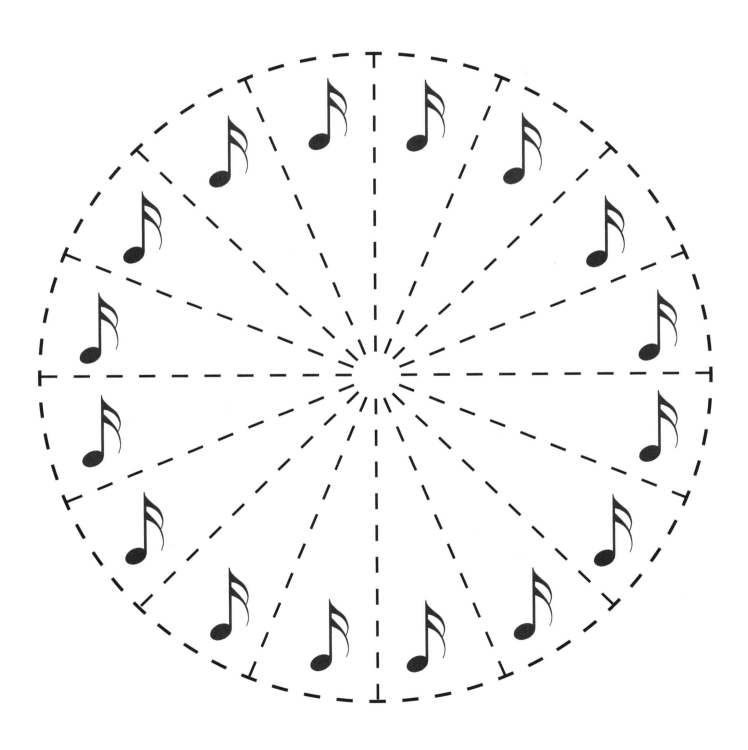

COUNTING

Quarter Notes: It is very easy to count notes once you can remember them. To count quarter notes in 4/4, say "**1, 2, 3, 4**." Clap along as you count.

8th Notes: These notes are counted like quarter notes, but with an "&" in between each numerical count: "**1 & 2 & 3 & 4 &**." Clap along as you count the 8th notes.

16th Notes: 16th notes are counted using an "e, &, a" in between the numbers, like this: "**1 e & a 2 e & a 3 e & a 4 e & a**." Clap along as you count the 16th notes.

When you put all of these together, you get the language of drums that looks like this:

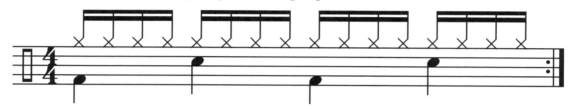

Clap along and count the following notes out loud. Listen to the different patterns. This is the foundation for all rhythm in music. Drummers use these patterns to make beats.

Quarter Notes

1 – 2 – 3 – 4 – 1 – 2 – 3 – 4

8th Notes

1 & 2 & 3 & 4 & 1 & 2 & 3 & 4 &

16th Notes

1 e & a 2 e & a 3 e & a 4 e & a

Download versions of the flash cards on the following pages at moderndrummer.com/fundamentalsofdrumming. Cut them out and cycle through them repeatedly to memorize the notation. (Page 29 = the front of the cards and page 30 = the back. Use the numbers in the bottom-right corner of the cards to match them up.)

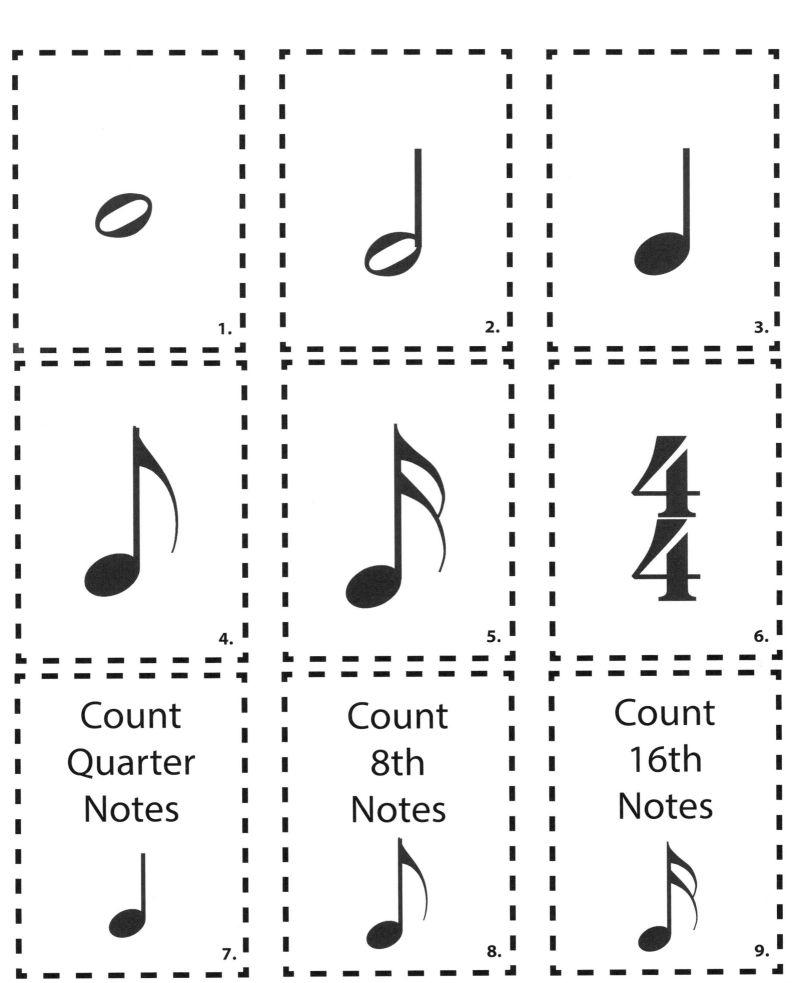

Quarter Note	Half Note	Whole Note
3.	2.	1.
Time Signature	16th Note	8th Note
6.	5.	4.
Count 16th Notes 1e&a2e&a 3e&a4e&a	Count 8th Notes 1&2&3&4&	Count Quarter Notes 1-2-3-4
9.	8.	7.

Music Notation Practice

Another way to help children memorize musical notation is to have them write it. Use this blank notation form and ask the student to randomly draw some of the notes you've discussed. Afterward, ask him or her to identify each note.

STRETCHES AND WARM-UPS

The drums are the most physical of all musical instruments, as they require the use of both large and small muscle groups. Drumming also requires a certain level of endurance. This means that the body must be loose in order for blood to flow properly to the muscles. Most professional drummers do special warm-up exercises before performing. Many of them have developed their own pre-show rituals. Proper posture is also very important for drummers. These physical preparations help to create a connection between the mind and body and allow the drummer to play safely and comfortably. Remember that a healthy drummer is a happy drummer!

Note: If students are familiar with body-stretching exercises from their school's physical education program, encourage them to use these routines as well. The following exercises represent drummer-specific stretches and warm-ups.

Some simple stretching exercises can be done using a pair of drumsticks.

Wrist Stretch

1. With both hands, grasp and hold both drumsticks in front of you, as if you were holding on to a roller coaster's safety bar. Gently bend your wrists down and up several times.
2. Now bend each wrist separately. First stretch the right, and then the left.

Hand Stretch

1. Extend your arm straight out in front of you, with your palm facing away and your fingers pointing up. Gently pull your fingertips back toward you with your other hand. Repeat the stretch with the opposite hand.
2. Extend your arm straight out in front of you, with your palm facing toward you and your fingers pointing down. Gently pull your fingertips toward you with your other hand. Repeat the stretch with the opposite hand.

Shoulder Stretch

1. Hold both drumsticks in one hand. Put them over your shoulder so that they are resting straight down the middle of your back. Reach behind with your other hand and grab the sticks behind your back. Now gently stretch by pulling the sticks upward. Repeat for both arms. Then repeat the process, but this time pull down on the sticks instead of up.

Note: The authors would like to emphasize the importance of safety and recommend that adults take the time to explain that a disregard for preparation or proper technique may result in painful injuries, including carpal tunnel syndrome and other repetitive-strain conditions. By relating the act of drumming to a sport, gym class, or recess, children may better understand the importance of warming up prior to playing. Safety first!

Rich's Warm-Up Routine

"I warm up for at least thirty minutes before every show. It gets the blood flowing, warms my muscles, and helps me get into the right state of mind to perform at my best."

The following sticking patterns are meant to be done on a practice pad. The purpose is to get the blood flowing properly and loosen up the arms, hands, and wrist muscles. Be sure to alternate between hands, working on the evenness of the strokes. Count along with each stroke while trying to maintain an even tempo. Start slowly, and then gradually increase the speed.

> **Quarter-Note Pattern** (repeat both patterns, alternating between hands)
>
> Right Hand: **1 – 2 – 3 – 4**
> Left Hand: **1 – 2 – 3 – 4**
>
> **8th-Note Pattern** (repeat both patterns, alternating between hands)
>
> Right Hand: **1 – & – 2 – & – 3 – & – 4 – &**
> Left Hand: **1 – & – 2 – & – 3 – & – 4 – &**

For the advanced player, try using the following quarter-, 8th-, and 16th-note combos.

R R R R   R R R R R R R R   R L R L R L R L R L R L R L R L

L L L L   L L L L L L L L   L R L R L R L R L R L R L R L R

FUNDAMENTALS PROGRAM

The exercises on the next few pages are designed to enable the child to progress from simple hand clapping and tabletop pattern playing to the drum pad and/or snare drum and finally to the drumkit. Some exercises will require adult participation and guidance, while others can be completed entirely by the child. We have developed this series of exercises, which can accompany most kinds of music, to be fun and familiar.

FUN and Done

Copy this page and check off each section as you complete it.

_____ Clapping Exercises: Upbeats and Downbeats

_____ Tapping Exercises: Mimicking Patterns

_____ Note Groupings

_____ Introduction to Rudiments

_____ Pattern Phrases

_____ The Dynamic Duo

_____ Pedal Exercises

_____ The Money Beats

_____ Foot Exercises

_____ Three-Way Independence

_____ Four-Way Independence

_____ Fun With Toms!

_____ 16th Notes

_____ "Pea Soup"

_____ World Beats

_____ Your First Drum Solo!

Paul Griffin

CLAPPING EXERCISES: UPBEATS AND DOWNBEATS

1. Begin this exercise by listening to music. It can be any kind of music you choose. (Most nursery rhymes and traditional rock 'n' roll songs work well, because they usually have a simple, recognizable beat.) Listen to the speed (or tempo) of the song. Is it a slow song or a fast song? After you finish listening to the whole song, listen to it again and try to clap along to the rhythmic beat.

2. Clap and count out loud: **"1-2-3-4."** Try to be consistent. Each number you count is a note or beat. In most popular music, **beats 1 and 3** are the **downbeats** of the song and **beats 2 and 4** are the **upbeats**, which are also called the **backbeat**.

3. Try clapping **1** and **3** louder than **2** and **4**. This highlights the downbeats by giving them louder claps than the upbeats. Do this for a few minutes.

4. Now try clapping the **2** and **4** louder than the **1** and **3**. This highlights the upbeats by giving them louder claps than the downbeats. Do this for a few minutes. You're not just clapping—you're clapping in time and making rhythm!

TAPPING EXERCISES: MIMICKING PATTERNS

1. [Adult] Sit facing the child. Rest your hands flat on a tabletop or on your knees.

2. [Adult] Try to tap basic rhythms with your hands, such as **"1-&-2-&-3-&-4-&."** Have the child mimic the sequence. Do this a few times until the child is comfortable. You may wish to make up your own patterns. Make it fun!

3. [Adult] You can remove beats from a sequence and insert a **rest**. For example, tap **"1-[rest]-3-4."** Begin with short sequences, up to four beats. Say the word *rest* in place of the corresponding number. Have the child mimic the sequence.

4. [Adult] As the child grasps this concept, add variety to your sequences by increasing the tempo (speed), lengthening the sequences, and adding more complex rhythms. The goal of this exercise is to enable the child to repeat simple beats learned by ear.

5. [Adult] As the child gains proficiency in playing rhythms on the table, begin adding simple rhythms that incorporate tapping with the foot. Have the child count and tap rhythms with the feet that land on beats **1** and **3**, while tapping rhythms with the hands that land on **2** and **4**.

HAND DRUMMING

Hand drumming was the earliest and most primitive form of percussion, and it is still used frequently in music today. **Hand drums** are played with the bare hand instead of a stick or mallet. The earliest types of hand drums were made from hollowed-out logs or clay pots with animal skins stretched over the top opening. These types of drums are played in cultures from all around the world and are often used to communicate and celebrate. Over time, hand drums have evolved into a variety of instruments that include tabla, bongos, congas, djembes, tambourines, cajons, and frame drums.

Here are a couple of modern hand drums descended from ancient instruments.

Djembe

Cajon

Students may be interested in playing a hand drum at this point. Hand drums can be a fun and affordable way to introduce children to percussion instruments prior to the drumset. Check them out!

NOTE GROUPINGS

The following exercises are designed to introduce the more advanced student to some simple grouping patterns. Each note depicted below represents a **right-hand (R)** or **left-hand (L)** tap. Each rest sign represents a pause between beats. Count out loud. (Refer to the previous counting exercises if necessary.) Play the exercises with bare hands on a hand drum like a conga or djembe, or use sticks on a pad or snare.

Quarter-Note Groupings

8th-Note Groupings

INTRODUCTION TO RUDIMENTS

A **rudiment** is a common pattern used in percussion music. These patterns can be played in many different ways to create all kinds of **rolls** and **fills**. Marching drum lines use rudiments to play cadences that keep the rest of the band in step.

This section presents a basic introduction to four rudiments and their crazy names, which come from the way they sound. The ability to play rudiments correctly depends on the amount of time they are practiced. Don't be discouraged. Even adult drummers have to practice rudiments many times before they become proficient.

All rudiments should be practiced at an even, moderate tempo. Just as we counted numbers aloud in previous exercises, have the student call out the **rights** and **lefts**.

Make sure the child is comfortable with the hand-tapping portion before moving on to the drum or pad. Rudiments are among the most frustrating of all drum exercises, so remember to encourage the student. Don't give up!

The following exercises have been broken down into two categories: hands and sticks. The patterns on the left are to be played by the hands on a flat surface such as a table. The same patterns, notated on the right, are to be played with sticks on a drum or pad.

HANDS *To be played on a flat surface such as a table*	STICKS *To be played on a drum pad or snare drum*
Single-Stroke Roll **R-L-R-L-R-L-R-L**	R L R L R L R L
Double-Stroke Roll **RR-LL-RR-LL-RR-LL-RR-LL**	RRLLRRLL
Paradiddle **R-L-RR-L-R-LL**	R L R R L R L L

Note: The goal is to have the child play all the strokes in a slow and steady rhythm. This process may take some time, so remember to make it fun!

PATTERN PHRASES

Another fun way to learn rudiments is to match them with familiar words and phrases. This system works very well for younger children. Both one- and two-syllable words can be used in place of **rights** and **lefts**. Simply match each word with a tap or strike. Find basic but familiar words that are easily repeated, and have the child say the word aloud in unison with each stroke as it is completed.

Single-Stroke Roll (R-L-R-L-R-L-R-L):

Mom-Dad-Mom-Dad-Mom-Dad-Mom-Dad...

Double-Stroke Roll (RR-LL-RR-LL-RR-LL-RR-LL):

Momma-Dadda-Momma-Dadda-Momma-Dadda-Momma-Dadda...

Paradiddle (R-L-R-R-L-R-L-L):

Mom-Dad-Mom-ma-Dad-Mom-Dad-da...

Flam (lR-rL):
Note: The larger word is struck/said louder. Play the smaller word just before the larger word.

Dad **Mom** - Mom**Dad**...

Using a Metronome

A metronome is a practice tool that produces a steady pulse to help musicians play rhythms accurately. The pulses are measured in beats per minute (bpm). Most metronomes are capable of playing beats from 35 to 250 bpm. Metronomes are helpful when practicing and learning to maintain an established tempo. As with everything, start with the metronome at a slow rate, and then increase the speed as the child becomes more comfortable playing the rudiments.

Timekeeping is a very important part of drumming. All drummers, no matter what kind of music they play, have to maintain a steady pace at some point. Many professional drummers play to a **click track** when performing, in order to keep the proper tempo.

THE DYNAMIC DUO

One of the most important keys to maturing as a drummer is the ability to play both loudly and softly. These contrasts in volume are called **dynamics**. As drummers become more comfortable at playing their instrument, they also play more dynamically. Drummers use dynamics to accent the rhythms within the music they're playing. Here's an exercise to try with the student.

1. **Use a drumstick as a pointer.**

2. **Position the book on a music stand, and open it to this page.**

3. **Ask the child to play a pattern at a normal, moderate volume.**

4. **Point to the LOUD ("forte") sign. The child should start to play louder.**

5. **Take the pointer away. The child should resume playing at a normal volume.**

6. **Point to the SOFT ("piano") sign. The child should start to play softer.**

7. **Repeat the process several times, transitioning from loud to normal to soft.**

8. **Try alternating back and forth between the two signs. Be sure to mix it up!**

(Remember to repeat this exercise later on, when the child plays the drumset.)

Note: "Piano" is the Italian word for "soft," and "forte" is the Italian word for "loud."

FOOT FOCUS

In the previous chapters we covered various lessons, including matched grip, note recognition, stretching, warm-ups, clapping and tapping exercises, rudiments, and pattern phrases. The student should be comfortable with those routines prior to continuing on to the drumset section of this book.

For the remainder of the book, we will focus on the use of the bass drum, snare drum, and hi-hat cymbals. These three instruments are the building blocks of all beats. That's the cake. Everything else is icing. It is recommended that the child start on a basic beginner's drumkit. As the child becomes more competent, you can add more gear. Be sure to adjust the drum and cymbal heights and placements so that they are comfortable for the child to reach.

Bass Drum Pedals

A wide variety of foot pedals is available to drummers today. This includes single and double pedals that allow the drummer to play with either foot. Drum manufacturing pioneer William F. Ludwig made the first functional bass drum pedal in 1909, paving the way for the modern drumkit. A doubled version came decades later and enabled drummers with a single bass drum to sound as if they were playing a drumkit with two bass drums.

The most common bass drum pedal is the **single pedal**. The first versions were made of wood and were operated using straps. Today's versions feature chain drives and hard or soft beaters that can be interchanged for different sounds.

The **double pedal** allows the drummer to play a single bass drum as if there were two. It operates with a second footplate controlling a second beater on the same drum.

Just as their hands are used to play the top of the drumset (snare, toms, and cymbals), drummers use their feet to play the bottom of the kit (hi-hat and bass drum). By stepping on the pedals, drummers are able to play the bass drum and open and close the hi-hat cymbals.

The bass drum pedal has a beater attached to it. This beater hits the bass drum head every time the drummer steps on the pedal. The bass drum creates the downbeat that is the foundation of the groove. The **groove** is the drummer's way of driving the song. Some drummers use two pedals with two bass drums. Others use double pedals that allow them to play one bass drum with two beaters. (Some heavy metal drummers play their double bass drums very fast!)

The hi-hat cymbals are also controlled by a pedal. They are usually set to be slightly open. This means the two cymbals are adjusted so as to avoid contact with one another when at rest. When the drummer steps down on the pedal, the hi-hats close together, like a clamshell. When the drummer lifts his or her foot off of the pedal, the hi-hats reopen. The drummer can play the hi-hats with a drumstick or open and close them with the pedal while playing other parts of the drumset with the sticks.

Foot Independence

Perhaps the biggest challenge for any drummer is learning how to use all four limbs simultaneously. After all, drummers are basically doing four different things at the same time. This action is called **independence**. Now that we have introduced several exercises to practice playing rhythms, patterns, and rudiments for the hands, the following exercises are designed specifically for the feet.

One of the earliest exercises introduced to kids in school is the activity of stomping. Whether marching in a parade or simply moving to music, the act of stepping in time is a familiar one. Using this simple approach, children can learn the coordination they'll need to work the pedals.

Note: It may help to set up the hi-hat cymbals and bass drum separately, so that the student can focus on his or her feet without the distraction of the rest of the drumset. Once students are comfortable working with their feet, you can slowly introduce other pieces of the drumset, starting with the snare drum.

This section uses the same counting philosophy that was introduced in the hand and stick exercises. At this point the student should be relatively familiar with them.

You may remember the following counting patterns from the earlier chapters. Just as you used numbers and words to tell your hands what to do, we will now apply them to your feet. Start out very slowly. Count the numbers or say the words *right* and *left* out loud. Be aware of what your feet are doing.

Exercise 1

Pattern 1: Play the bass drum and hi-hat pedals in unison: **1-2-3-4** (repeat)
Pattern 2: Bass drum only (single beats): **1-2-3-4** (repeat)
Pattern 3: Hi-hat only (use both tight closed and splashy open sounds): **1-2-3-4** (repeat)
Pattern 4: Alternate bass drum and hi-hat (walking pace): **R-L-R-L-R-L-R-L** (repeat)
Pattern 5: Double up the bass drum so it plays two notes twice as fast as the left:
RR-L-RR-L-RR-L-RR-L (repeat)

It may help to present these exercises as a march. Have the child sit in a chair, away from the drums completely, and work through the above patterns by simply stomping the feet on the ground. Tell him or her to imagine leading a parade, and that each step is a marching step. This will get the child alternating between the bass drum foot and hi-hat foot without any distraction.

Once the student is comfortable with these patterns, move on to the actual pedals and repeat the process. The goal is to have the child alternating between the two pedals in a slow, steady rhythm. This may take some time to master, so remember to make it fun!

Here are the same exercises without the pedals.

Exercise 2

Pattern 1: Both feet stomping together in unison: **1-2-3-4** (repeat)
Pattern 2: Right foot: **1-2-3-4** (repeat)
Pattern 3: Left foot: **1-2-3-4** (repeat)
Pattern 4: Alternate between the right and left foot: **R-L-R-L-R-L-R-L** (repeat)
Pattern 5: Double up on the right foot: **RR-L-RR-L-RR-L-RR-L** (repeat)

Here are similar foot patterns written in music notation. Note how they are broken down into three parts: bass drum (right foot), hi-hat (left foot), and bass drum and hi-hat (unison).

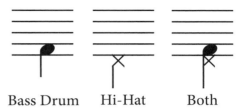

Bass Drum   Hi-Hat   Both

Play the following bass drum and hi-hat patterns. Count each beat out loud.

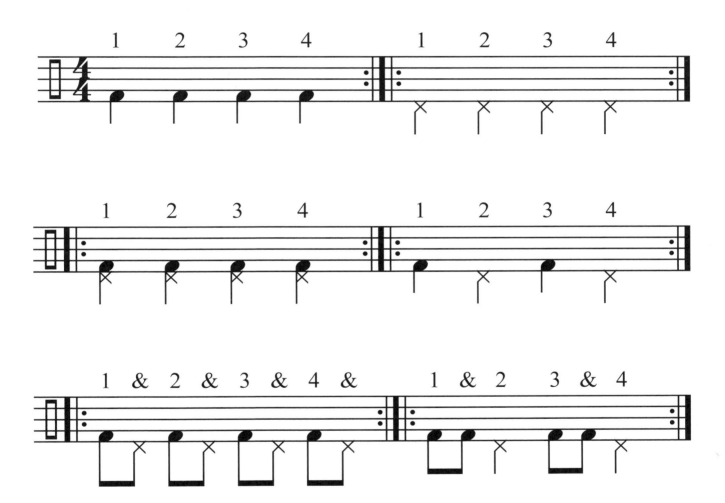

Before you continue…

The goal of *FUNdamentals of Drumming for Kids* is to make learning *fun!* The drumset portion of this program is perhaps the most challenging. Remember to encourage students to enjoy themselves. No one ever became a drummer because he or she didn't like playing the drums. Drumming is all about feel. If the drummer feels great, the band feels great. And if the band feels great, the audience feels great. It all starts with the drummer!

THE MONEY BEATS
"Play it like you say it!"

Here's a collection of exercises, called the "Money Beats," that mimic the **grooves** every drummer should know in order to play music professionally. As they are the building blocks for most other beats, we are including a brief introduction here. These five fun beats are the grooves on which most popular music is based.

Money Beat #1, Boom – Smack: Play straight quarter or 8th notes on the hi-hat, with the bass drum hitting on beats 1 and 3 and the snare drum hitting on beats 2 and 4. Play it like you say it: *"BOOM – SMACK – BOOM – SMACK – BOOM – SMACK – BOOM – SMACK."*

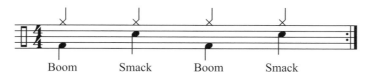

Money Beat #2, the Heartbeat: This is just like Money Beat #1 but with a second bass drum hit added on the & of beat 2. Think of the rhythm of your heartbeat. Play it like you say it: *"BOOM – SMACK BOOM BOOM – SMACK BOOM BOOM – SMACK BOOM BOOM – SMACK BOOM."*

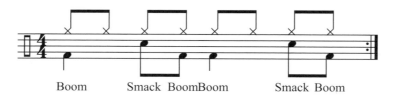

Money Beat #3, Classic Rock Beat: Similar to Money Beat #2 but with the bass drum hits shifted to beat 3 and the & of beat 3. Play it like you say it: *"BOOM – SMACK – BOOM BOOM – SMACK – BOOM – SMACK – BOOM BOOM – SMACK."*

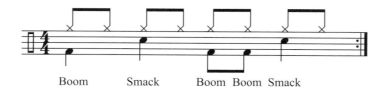

Money Beat #4, We Will Rock Ya': This familiar beat puts two bass drum hits before the snare, on the & of beats 1 and 3, with the snare staying on beats 2 and 4. Play it like you say it: *"BOOM BOOM – SMACK – BOOM BOOM – SMACK – BOOM BOOM – SMACK – BOOM BOOM – SMACK."*

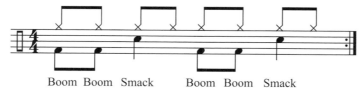

Money Beat #5, Four on the Floor: This pattern has the bass drum on all four beats, with the snare hitting on beats 2 and 4. Play it like you say it: *"BOOM – BOCK – BOOM – BOCK – BOOM – BOCK – BOOM – BOCK."*

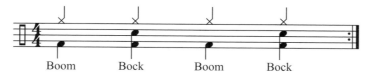

ALONE AND TOGETHER

In order to play a set of drums, drummers must develop the ability to do four different things—with four different limbs—all at the same time! Although that may sound like something you might see at a circus, it's quite easy once you train your body. Much as with the previous exercises, this process may take some time, but it will eventually become second nature if students practice to the point where they develop **mental and muscle memory**. This is also the point where the relationships between the hands and feet are developed. One key factor in building four-way independence is knowing when to strike the drums and/or cymbals **alone** and when to strike them **together**.

Alone is when the limb plays a beat without any other limb playing at the same time. (Example: hitting the bass drum while the other three limbs rest on the beat.) **Together** is when two or more limbs play at the same time. (Example: hitting the hi-hat and snare on the beat.) As you progress through the exercises, it may help to break down those counts to figure out which beats are played alone and which are played together.

Translation Table Key

For all of the following exercises, both traditional musical notation and our *FUNdamentals* translation will be presented for use depending on the student's level of playing and overall comprehension. Younger children may wish to begin with the tables, with the intention to transition to the notated versions as they become more advanced.

The top row of the table provides the count. The rows below represent a piece of the drumset and on which count(s) to play it. All exercises are written for a four-piece set with two toms.

8th-Note Count	1	&	2	&	3	&	4	&
Hi-Hat	H	H	H	H	H	H	H	H
Tom 1				T1				
Snare			S				S	
Tom 2								T2
Bass	B					B		

RECOMMENDATIONS

The three key factors to remember about drumming are **time, tone, and technique.** The drummer's most important role is to maintain a steady count (timing) for the rest of the band. Tone involves not only the quality of sound of the instrument but also the way you draw sound from it with your touch. Technique dictates how well you perform with your instrument. These are referred to as the **Three T's**. They all relate to each other, and they feed one another. Playing with great technique helps your tone, while doing it all with great timing is what makes a good drummer great.

Students

- Be sure to count when you're playing/practicing. It may help to count out loud. Play with a metronome. If you do not have a metronome, there are many metronome applications available as a free download on the Internet. Start out slowly and speed up as you become more comfortable with the flow and feel of each exercise.

- Build your **musical memory**. This is a combination of physical and mental memory that comes with repetitive practice. Eventually you won't have to think about the mechanics of drumming. Then you can concentrate on the groove.

- The Money Beats are based on the most popular grooves that you will likely play with a band. It's very important to get to know—and feel—these beats inside and out. They not only help keep the band steady, but they also often act as the heartbeat of the song.

- Focus on playing evenly, and have fun! Feel it!

Parents/Teachers

- After the students are comfortable with reading and playing through the charts, ask them to add a little attitude to the patterns by using different tempos (speeds) and dynamics. Every drummer is unique, and his or her personality should radiate when he or she plays.

- Remind the child to always play the bass drum and snare with power, as they are the foundation of the beat. More advanced players may wish to try playing the snare drum with a rimshot (hitting the stick across the snare drumhead and rim simultaneously) and using a variety of accents on the hi-hat cymbals. This helps express different feels and attitudes.

FOOT EXERCISES

To get started on the drumset, have the student play the bass drum parts from the Money Beats by themselves.

Ex. 1

8th-Note Count	1	&	2	&	3	&	4	&
Bass Drum	B				B			

Ex. 2

8th-Note Count	1	&	2	&	3	&	4	&
Bass Drum	B			B	B			

Ex. 3

8th-Note Count	1	&	2	&	3	&	4	&
Bass Drum	B			B	B			B

Ex. 4

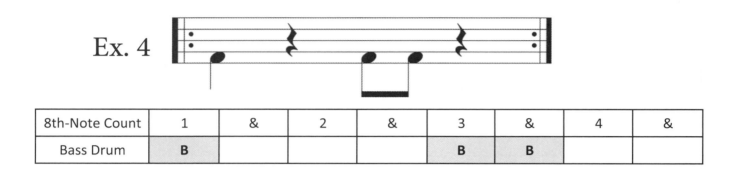

8th-Note Count	1	&	2	&	3	&	4	&
Bass Drum	B				B	B		

Ex. 5

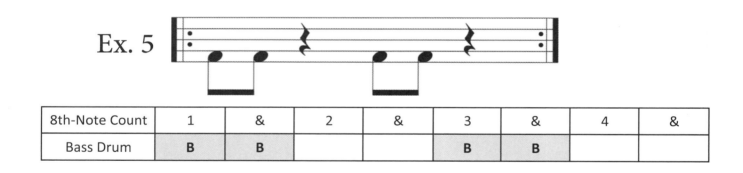

8th-Note Count	1	&	2	&	3	&	4	&
Bass Drum	B	B			B	B		

Ex. 6

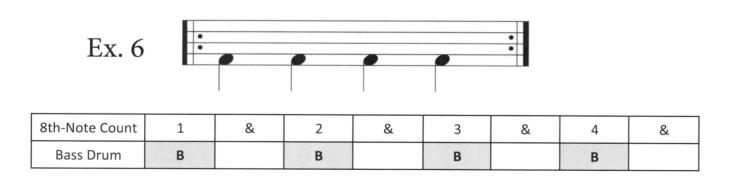

8th-Note Count	1	&	2	&	3	&	4	&
Bass Drum	B		B		B		B	

Add the Hi-Hat

Now let's add the hi-hat foot on beats 2 and 4 to each of the previous bass drum patterns.

Ex. 7

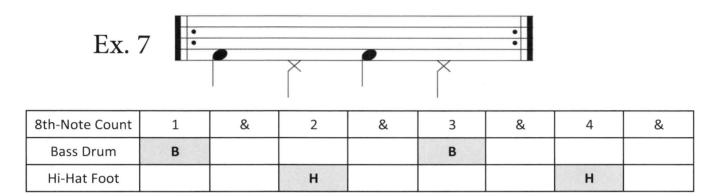

8th-Note Count	1	&	2	&	3	&	4	&
Bass Drum	B				B			
Hi-Hat Foot			H				H	

Ex. 8

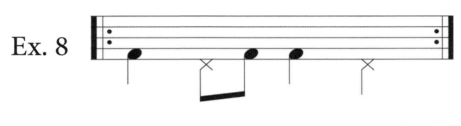

8th-Note Count	1	&	2	&	3	&	4	&
Bass Drum	B			B	B			
Hi-Hat Foot			H				H	

Ex. 9

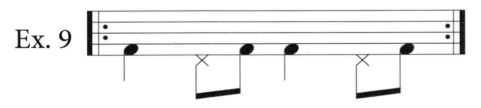

8th-Note Count	1	&	2	&	3	&	4	&
Bass Drum	B			B	B			B
Hi-Hat Foot			H				H	

Ex. 10

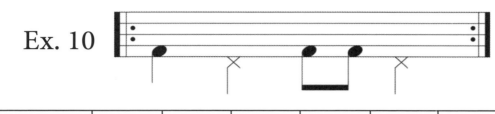

8th-Note Count	1	&	2	&	3	&	4	&
Bass Drum	B				B	B		
Hi-Hat Foot			H				H	

Ex. 11

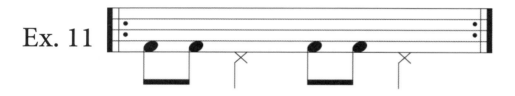

8th-Note Count	1	&	2	&	3	&	4	&
Bass Drum	B	B			B	B		
Hi-Hat Foot			H				H	

Ex. 12

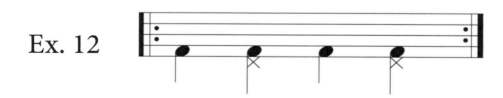

8th-Note Count	1	&	2	&	3	&	4	&
Bass Drum	B		B		B		B	
Hi-Hat Foot			H				H	

Now that your feet are ready, let's move on!

THREE-WAY INDEPENDENCE

Now let's work on three-way independence (three limbs playing at once). Begin by playing quarter notes on the hi-hat with the stick.

Ex. 1

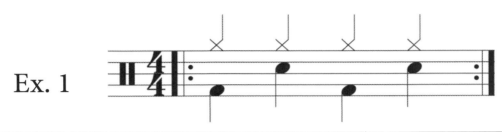

8th-Note Count	1	&	2	&	3	&	4	&
Hi-Hat	H		H		H		H	
Snare			S				S	
Bass Drum	B				B			

Ex. 2

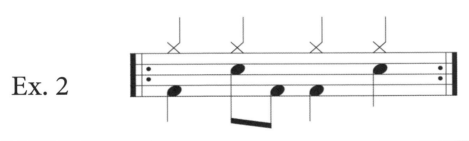

8th-Note Count	1	&	2	&	3	&	4	&
Hi-Hat	H		H		H		H	
Snare			S				S	
Bass Drum	B			B	B			

Ex. 3

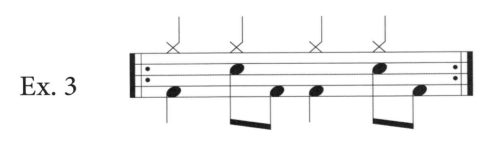

8th-Note Count	1	&	2	&	3	&	4	&
Hi-Hat	H		H		H		H	
Snare			S				S	
Bass Drum	B			B	B			B

Ex. 4

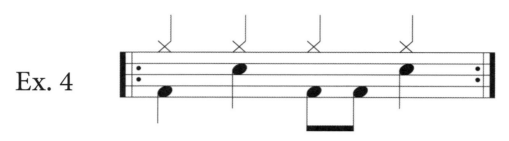

8th-Note Count	1	&	2	&	3	&	4	&
Hi-Hat	H		H		H		H	
Snare			S				S	
Bass Drum	B				B	B		

Ex. 5

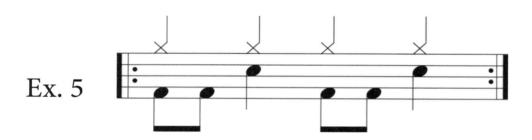

8th-Note Count	1	&	2	&	3	&	4	&
Hi-Hat	H		H		H		H	
Snare			S				S	
Bass Drum	B	B			B	B		

Ex. 6

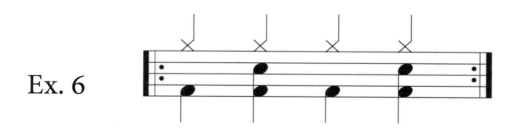

8th-Note Count	1	&	2	&	3	&	4	&
Hi-Hat	H		H		H		H	
Snare			S				S	
Bass Drum	B		B		B		B	

Now let's play the previous grooves with 8th notes on the hi-hat.

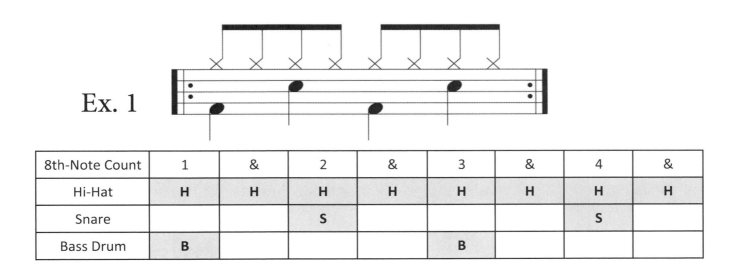

Ex. 1

8th-Note Count	1	&	2	&	3	&	4	&
Hi-Hat	H	H	H	H	H	H	H	H
Snare			S				S	
Bass Drum	B				B			

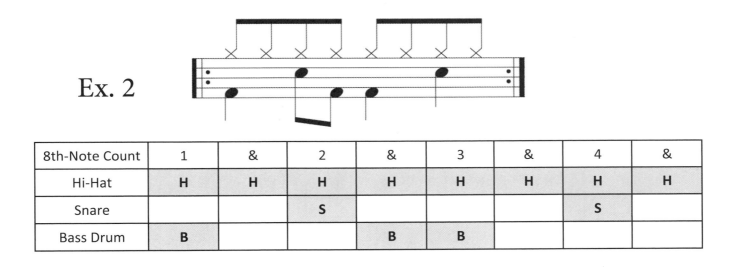

Ex. 2

8th-Note Count	1	&	2	&	3	&	4	&
Hi-Hat	H	H	H	H	H	H	H	H
Snare			S				S	
Bass Drum	B			B	B			

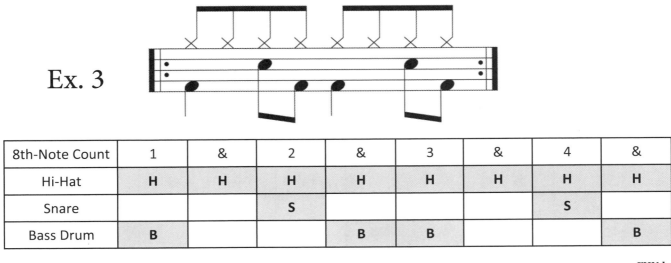

Ex. 3

8th-Note Count	1	&	2	&	3	&	4	&
Hi-Hat	H	H	H	H	H	H	H	H
Snare			S				S	
Bass Drum	B			B	B			B

Ex. 4

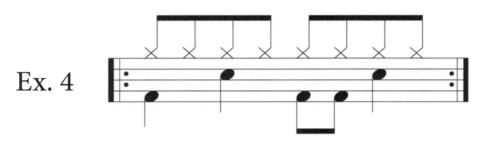

8th-Note Count	1	&	2	&	3	&	4	&
Hi-Hat	H	H	H	H	H	H	H	H
Snare			S				S	
Bass Drum	B					B	B	

Ex. 5

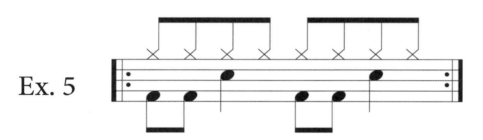

8th-Note Count	1	&	2	&	3	&	4	&
Hi-Hat	H	H	H	H	H	H	H	H
Snare			S				S	
Bass Drum	B	B			B	B		

Ex. 6

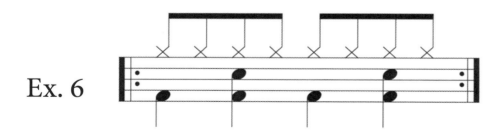

8th-Note Count	1	&	2	&	3	&	4	&
Hi-Hat	H	H	H	H	H	H	H	H
Snare			S				S	
Bass Drum	B		B		B		B	

More Three-Way Independence Exercises

In this next group of three-way independence grooves, the snare drum changes from just the backbeat to 8th-note variations. Again, begin by playing quarter notes on the hi-hat.

Ex. 1

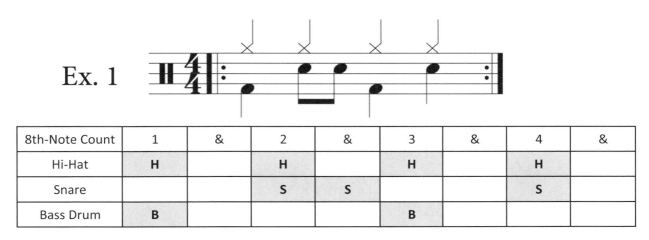

8th-Note Count	1	&	2	&	3	&	4	&
Hi-Hat	H		H		H		H	
Snare			S	S			S	
Bass Drum	B				B			

Ex. 2

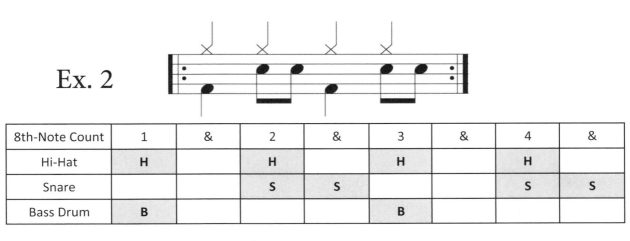

8th-Note Count	1	&	2	&	3	&	4	&
Hi-Hat	H		H		H		H	
Snare			S	S			S	S
Bass Drum	B				B			

Ex. 3

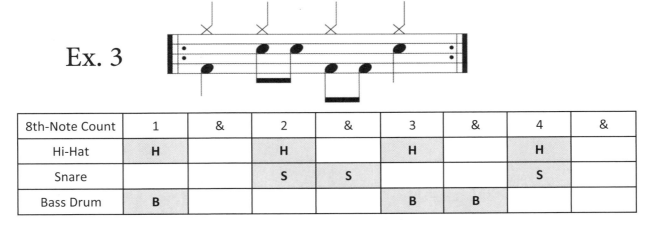

8th-Note Count	1	&	2	&	3	&	4	&
Hi-Hat	H		H		H		H	
Snare			S	S			S	
Bass Drum	B				B	B		

Ex. 4

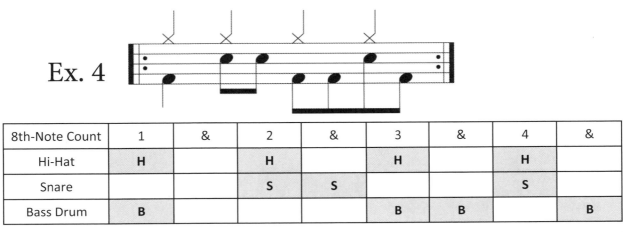

8th-Note Count	1	&	2	&	3	&	4	&
Hi-Hat	H		H		H		H	
Snare			S	S			S	
Bass Drum	B				B	B		B

Ex. 5

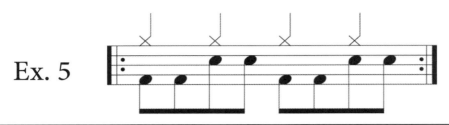

8th-Note Count	1	&	2	&	3	&	4	&
Hi-Hat	H		H		H		H	
Snare			S	S			S	S
Bass Drum	B	B			B	B		

Ex. 6

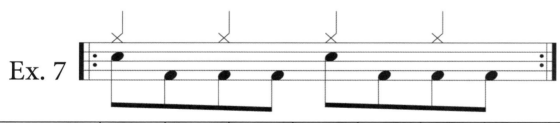

8th-Note Count	1	&	2	&	3	&	4	&
Hi-Hat	H		H		H		H	
Snare		S	S			S	S	
Bass Drum	B			B	B			B

Ex. 7

8th-Note Count	1	&	2	&	3	&	4	&
Hi-Hat	H		H		H		H	
Snare	S				S			
Bass Drum		B	B	B		B	B	B

Ex. 8

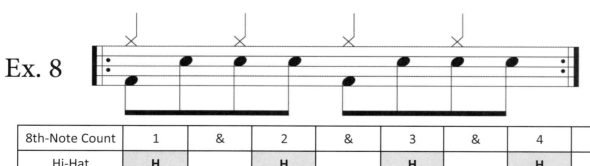

8th-Note Count	1	&	2	&	3	&	4	&
Hi-Hat	H		H		H		H	
Snare		S	S	S		S	S	S
Bass Drum	B				B			

Now let's play the grooves with 8th notes on the hi-hat.

Ex. 1

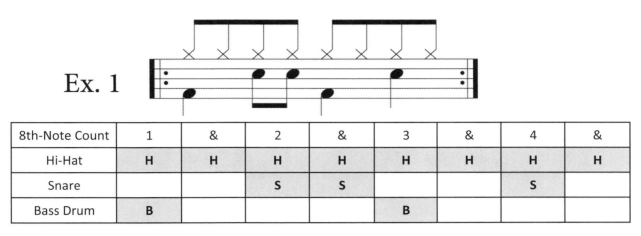

8th-Note Count	1	&	2	&	3	&	4	&
Hi-Hat	H	H	H	H	H	H	H	H
Snare			S	S			S	
Bass Drum	B				B			

Ex. 2

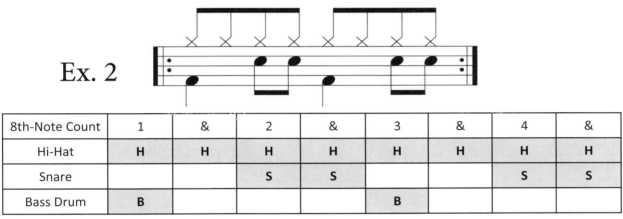

8th-Note Count	1	&	2	&	3	&	4	&
Hi-Hat	H	H	H	H	H	H	H	H
Snare			S	S			S	S
Bass Drum	B				B			

Ex. 3

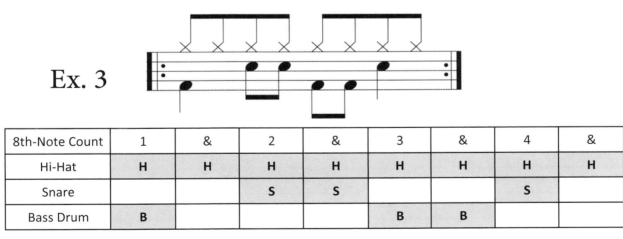

8th-Note Count	1	&	2	&	3	&	4	&
Hi-Hat	H	H	H	H	H	H	H	H
Snare			S	S			S	
Bass Drum	B				B	B		

Ex. 4

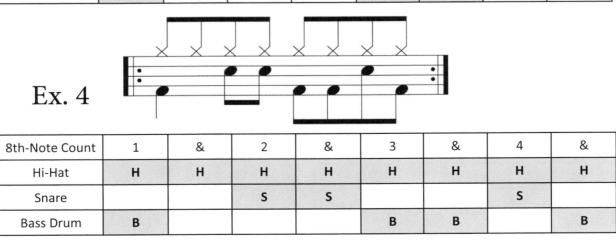

8th-Note Count	1	&	2	&	3	&	4	&
Hi-Hat	H	H	H	H	H	H	H	H
Snare			S	S			S	
Bass Drum	B				B	B		B

Ex. 5

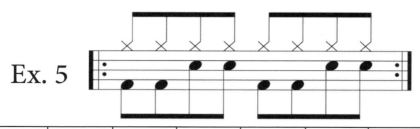

8th-Note Count	1	&	2	&	3	&	4	&
Hi-Hat	H	H	H	H	H	H	H	H
Snare			S	S			S	S
Bass Drum	B	B			B	B		

Ex. 6

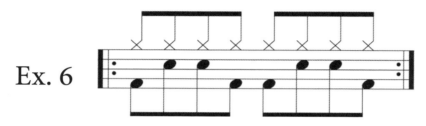

8th-Note Count	1	&	2	&	3	&	4	&
Hi-Hat	H	H	H	H	H	H	H	H
Snare		S	S			S	S	
Bass Drum	B			B	B			B

Ex. 7

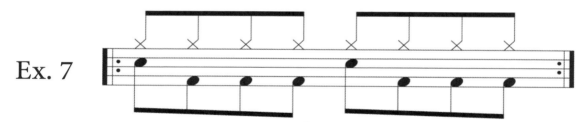

8th-Note Count	1	&	2	&	3	&	4	&
Hi-Hat	H	H	H	H	H	H	H	H
Snare	S				S			
Bass Drum		B	B	B		B	B	B

Ex. 8

8th-Note Count	1	&	2	&	3	&	4	&
Hi-Hat	H	H	H	H	H	H	H	H
Snare		S	S	S		S	S	S
Bass Drum	B				B			

FOUR-WAY INDEPENDENCE

Now let's get all four limbs involved. Start by playing the hi-hat with the foot on beats 2 and 4.

Ex. 1

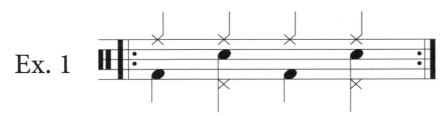

8th-Note Count	1	&	2	&	3	&	4	&
Ride	RC		RC		RC		RC	
Snare			S				S	
Bass Drum	B				B			
Hi-Hat Foot			H				H	

Ex. 2

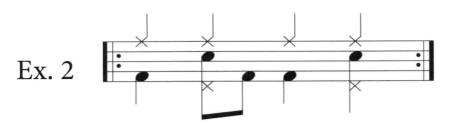

8th-Note Count	1	&	2	&	3	&	4	&
Ride	RC		RC		RC		RC	
Snare			S				S	
Bass Drum	B			B	B			
Hi-Hat Foot			H				H	

Ex. 3

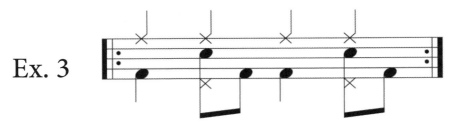

8th-Note Count	1	&	2	&	3	&	4	&
Ride	RC		RC		RC		RC	
Snare			S				S	
Bass Drum	B			B	B			B
Hi-Hat Foot			H				H	

Ex. 4

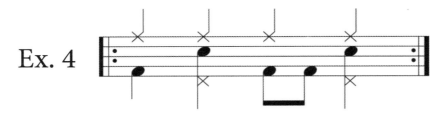

8th-Note Count	1	&	2	&	3	&	4	&
Ride	RC		RC		RC		RC	
Snare			S				S	
Bass Drum	B				B	B		
Hi-Hat Foot			H				H	

Ex. 5

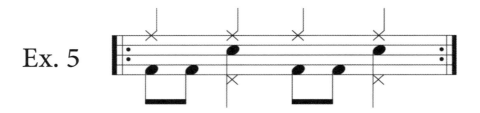

8th-Note Count	1	&	2	&	3	&	4	&
Ride	RC		RC		RC		RC	
Snare			S				S	
Bass Drum	B	B			B	B		
Hi-Hat Foot			H				H	

Ex. 6

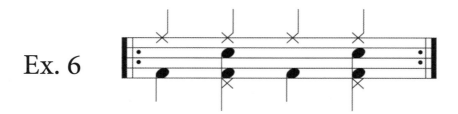

8th-Note Count	1	&	2	&	3	&	4	&
Ride	RC		RC		RC		RC	
Snare			S				S	
Bass Drum	B		B		B		B	
Hi-Hat Foot			H				H	

Now let's play those same grooves with the hi-hat foot playing quarter notes.

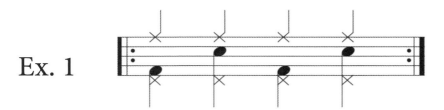

Ex. 1

8th-Note Count	1	&	2	&	3	&	4	&
Ride	RC		RC		RC		RC	
Snare			S				S	
Bass Drum	B				B			
Hi-Hat Foot	H		H		H		H	

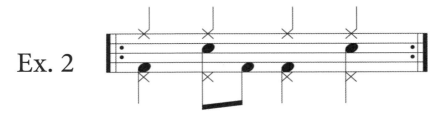

Ex. 2

8th-Note Count	1	&	2	&	3	&	4	&
Ride	RC		RC		RC		RC	
Snare			S				S	
Bass Drum	B			B	B			
Hi-Hat Foot	H		H		H		H	

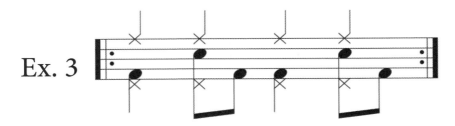

Ex. 3

8th-Note Count	1	&	2	&	3	&	4	&
Ride	RC		RC		RC		RC	
Snare			S				S	
Bass Drum	B			B	B			B
Hi-Hat Foot	H		H		H		H	

Ex. 4

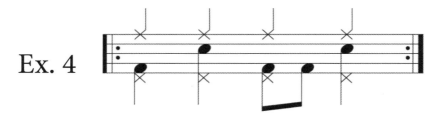

8th-Note Count	1	&	2	&	3	&	4	&
Ride	RC		RC		RC		RC	
Snare			S				S	
Bass Drum	B				B	B		
Hi-Hat Foot	H		H		H		H	

Ex. 5

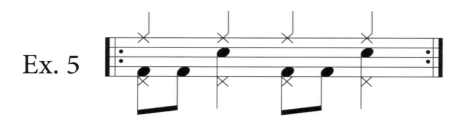

8th-Note Count	1	&	2	&	3	&	4	&
Ride	RC		RC		RC		RC	
Snare			S				S	
Bass Drum	B	B			B	B		
Hi-Hat Foot	H		H		H		H	

Ex. 6

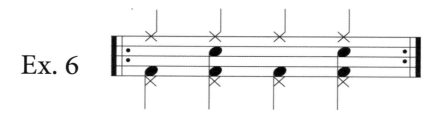

8th-Note Count	1	&	2	&	3	&	4	&
Ride	RC		RC		RC		RC	
Snare			S				S	
Bass Drum	B		B		B		B	
Hi-Hat Foot	H		H		H		H	

The beats in the next batch have 8th notes on the ride, while the hi-hat foot plays 2 and 4.

Ex. 1

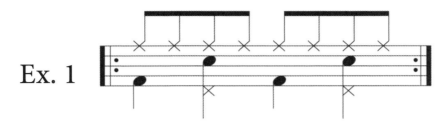

8th-Note Count	1	&	2	&	3	&	4	&
Ride	RC	RC	RC	RC	RC	RC	RC	RC
Snare			S				S	
Bass Drum	B				B			
Hi-Hat Foot			H				H	

Ex. 2

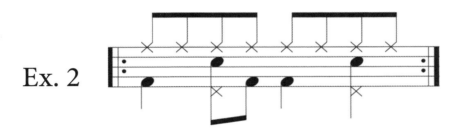

8th-Note Count	1	&	2	&	3	&	4	&
Ride	RC	RC	RC	RC	RC	RC	RC	RC
Snare			S				S	
Bass Drum	B			B	B			
Hi-Hat Foot			H				H	

Ex. 3

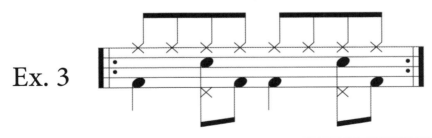

8th-Note Count	1	&	2	&	3	&	4	&
Ride	RC	RC	RC	RC	RC	RC	RC	RC
Snare			S				S	
Bass Drum	B			B	B			B
Hi-Hat Foot			H				H	

Ex. 4

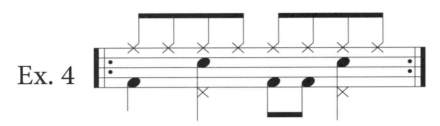

8th-Note Count	1	&	2	&	3	&	4	&
Ride	RC	RC	RC	RC	RC	RC	RC	RC
Snare			S				S	
Bass Drum	B					B	B	
Hi-Hat Foot			H				H	

Ex. 5

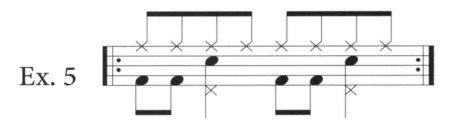

8th-Note Count	1	&	2	&	3	&	4	&
Ride	RC	RC	RC	RC	RC	RC	RC	RC
Snare			S				S	
Bass Drum	B	B			B	B		
Hi-Hat Foot			H				H	

Ex. 6

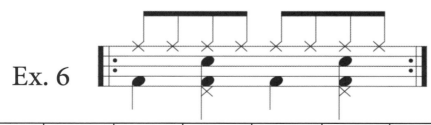

8th-Note Count	1	&	2	&	3	&	4	&
Ride	RC	RC	RC	RC	RC	RC	RC	RC
Snare			S				S	
Bass Drum	B		B		B		B	
Hi-Hat Foot			H				H	

Now let's play the grooves with the hi-hat foot playing quarter notes.

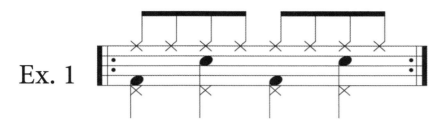

Ex. 1

8th-Note Count	1	&	2	&	3	&	4	&
Ride	RC	RC	RC	RC	RC	RC	RC	RC
Snare			S				S	
Bass Drum	B				B			
Hi-Hat Foot	H		H		H		H	

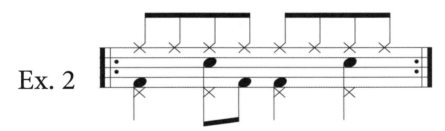

Ex. 2

8th-Note Count	1	&	2	&	3	&	4	&
Ride	RC	RC	RC	RC	RC	RC	RC	RC
Snare			S				S	
Bass Drum	B			B	B			
Hi-Hat Foot	H		H		H		H	

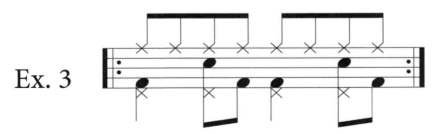

Ex. 3

8th-Note Count	1	&	2	&	3	&	4	&
Ride	RC	RC	RC	RC	RC	RC	RC	RC
Snare			S				S	
Bass Drum	B			B	B			B
Hi-Hat Foot	H		H		H		H	

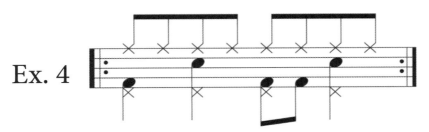

Ex. 4

8th-Note Count	1	&	2	&	3	&	4	&
Ride	RC	RC	RC	RC	RC	RC	RC	RC
Snare			S				S	
Bass Drum	B				B	B		
Hi-Hat Foot	H		H		H		H	

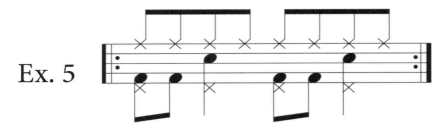

Ex. 5

8th-Note Count	1	&	2	&	3	&	4	&
Ride	RC	RC	RC	RC	RC	RC	RC	RC
Snare			S				S	
Bass Drum	B	B			B	B		
Hi-Hat Foot	H		H		H		H	

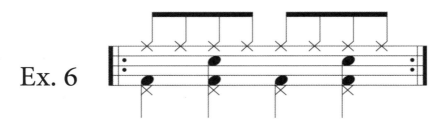

Ex. 6

8th-Note Count	1	&	2	&	3	&	4	&
Ride	RC	RC	RC	RC	RC	RC	RC	RC
Snare			S				S	
Bass Drum	B		B		B		B	
Hi-Hat Foot	H		H		H		H	

FUN WITH TOMS!

The tom-tom is believed to be one of the first constructed instruments used by early man for long-distance communication. It evolved into the drumkit in the twentieth century.

Although the term **tom-tom** is a British word for a child's toy drum, the name can also be found in the Anglo-Indian language. The tom comes from ancient cultures that used different combinations of primitive drums, often covered in animal skins, to communicate between tribes and villages. Most likely these early percussion instruments evolved from the clapping of hands and banging stones together. As civilizations evolved, so did the tom.

The first drumkit toms had no rims, and the heads were tacked to the shell. In the 1930s, drumset pioneers streamlined trapkits into a basic four-piece configuration comprising a bass drum, a snare, a small tom, and a larger tom. In time, legs were fitted to the larger toms (called "floor toms") and **consolettes** were invented to hang smaller toms over the bass drum. As major drum manufacturers began to offer tunable toms with hoops and tuning lugs, a variety of drums evolved into what we now call rack toms, floor toms, power toms, concert toms, gong bass drums, and so on. During the early days of the drumkit, drummers used only a few toms, and some had none at all. Several decades later, drummers began surrounding themselves with multiple toms of varying sizes and shapes. Some drummers used so many toms on their drumsets that the kits wrapped all the way around them. The highly innovative drummer Terry Bozzio uses a massive drumset, called the SS Bozzio, that includes twenty-six toms that are specially tuned. This allows him to create melodic musical compositions that are played entirely on the drums.

In this section we're going to experiment with different ways to incorporate the toms in drum fills, which are rhythms that drummers often play at the ends of song phrases to transition to a new section.

Begin by practicing each fill by itself. Then try playing one bar of a groove before the fill, or play three bars of a groove before the fill. Here are three examples of how to apply the fills in that context.

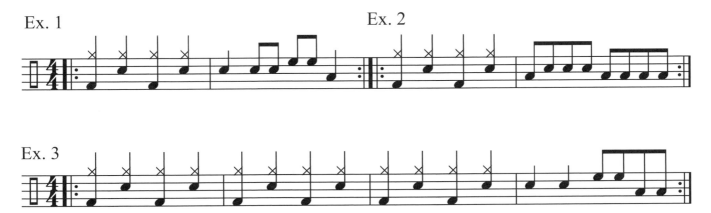

Ex. 1   Ex. 2

Ex. 3

Now it's time to get used to moving around the drumset. Here is a series of tom fills to practice.

Ex. 1

8th-Note Count	1	&	2	&	3	&	4	&
Tom 1					T1			
Snare	S		S					
Tom 2						T2		

Ex. 2

8th-Note Count	1	&	2	&	3	&	4	&
Tom 1					T1	T1		
Snare	S		S					
Tom 2							T2	

Ex. 3

8th-Note Count	1	&	2	&	3	&	4	&
Tom 1					T1	T1		
Snare	S		S					
Tom 2							T2	T2

Ex. 4

8th-Note Count	1	&	2	&	3	&	4	&
Tom 1					T1	T1		
Snare	S		S	S				
Tom 2							T2	

Ex. 5

8th-Note Count	1	&	2	&	3	&	4	&
Tom 1					T1	T1		
Snare	S		S	S				
Tom 2							T2	T2

Ex. 6

8th-Note Count	1	&	2	&	3	&	4	&
Tom 1					T1	T1		
Snare	S	S	S	S				
Tom 2							T2	T2

Ex. 7

8th-Note Count	1	&	2	&	3	&	4	&
Tom 1							T1	T1
Snare	S	S	S	S	S	S		

Ex. 8

8th-Note Count	1	&	2	&	3	&	4	&
Snare	S	S	S	S	S	S		
Tom 2							T2	T2

Ex. 9

8th-Note Count	1	&	2	&	3	&	4	&
Tom 1					T1	T1	T1	T1
Snare	S	S	S	S				

Ex. 10

8th-Note Count	1	&	2	&	3	&	4	&
Snare	S	S	S	S				
Tom 2					T2	T2	T2	T2

Ex. 11

8th-Note Count	1	&	2	&	3	&	4	&
Tom 1	T1							
Snare		S	S	S		S	S	S
Tom 2					T2			

Ex. 12

8th-Note Count	1	&	2	&	3	&	4	&
Tom 1			T1	T1				
Snare	S	S			S	S		
Tom 2							T2	T2

16TH NOTES

When you divide a quarter note into four parts, you get what's called 16th notes. (They're called 16th notes because there are sixteen of them in a measure of 4/4.)

Let's begin by practicing a few common 16th-note rhythms by themselves on the snare drum.

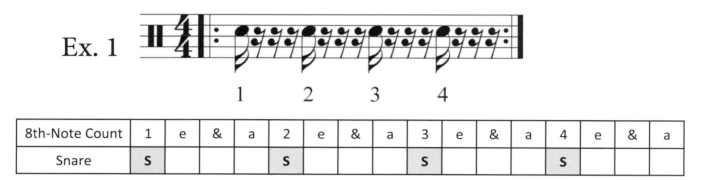

8th-Note Count	1	e	&	a	2	e	&	a	3	e	&	a	4	e	&	a
Snare	S				S				S				S			

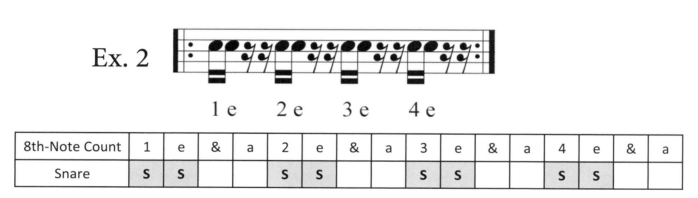

8th-Note Count	1	e	&	a	2	e	&	a	3	e	&	a	4	e	&	a
Snare	S	S			S	S			S	S			S	S		

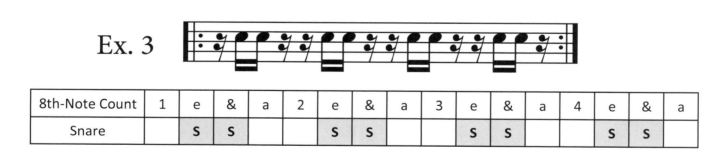

8th-Note Count	1	e	&	a	2	e	&	a	3	e	&	a	4	e	&	a
Snare		S	S			S	S			S	S			S	S	

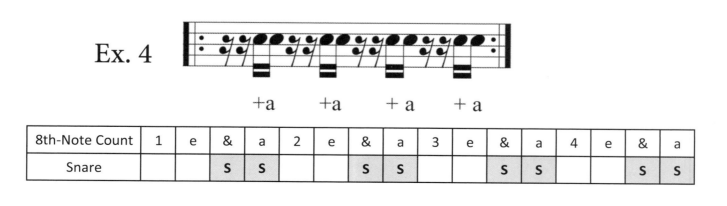

8th-Note Count	1	e	&	a	2	e	&	a	3	e	&	a	4	e	&	a
Snare			S	S			S	S			S	S			S	S

Ex. 5

1   a 2   a 3   a 4   a

8th-Note Count	1	e	&	a	2	e	&	a	3	e	&	a	4	e	&	a
Snare	S			S	S			S	S			S	S			S

Ex. 6

1   + a 2   + a 3   + a 4   + a

8th-Note Count	1	e	&	a	2	e	&	a	3	e	&	a	4	e	&	a
Snare	S		S	S	S		S	S	S		S	S	S		S	S

Ex. 7

1 e +   2 e +   3 e +   4 e +

8th-Note Count	1	e	&	a	2	e	&	a	3	e	&	a	4	e	&	a
Snare	S	S	S		S	S	S		S	S	S		S	S	S	

Ex. 8

1 e   a 2 e   a 3 e   a 4 e   a

8th-Note Count	1	e	&	a	2	e	&	a	3	e	&	a	4	e	&	a
Snare	S	S		S	S	S		S	S	S		S	S	S		

Here are a few ways to apply 16th-note rhythms to basic rock beats with 8th notes on the hi-hat.

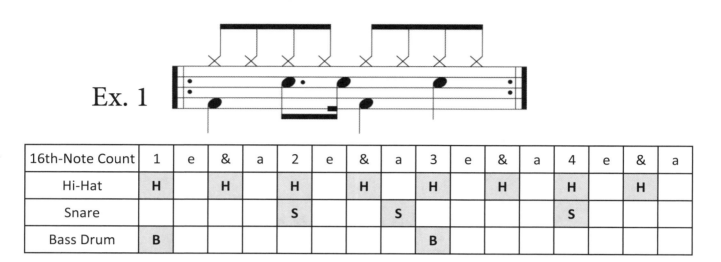

Ex. 1

16th-Note Count	1	e	&	a	2	e	&	a	3	e	&	a	4	e	&	a
Hi-Hat	H		H		H		H		H		H		H		H	
Snare					S			S					S			
Bass Drum	B								B							

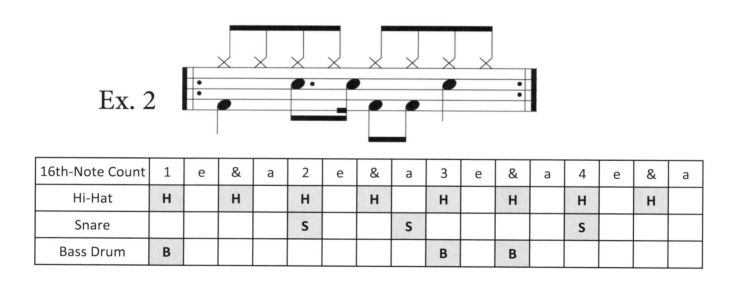

Ex. 2

16th-Note Count	1	e	&	a	2	e	&	a	3	e	&	a	4	e	&	a
Hi-Hat	H		H		H		H		H		H		H		H	
Snare					S			S					S			
Bass Drum	B									B		B				

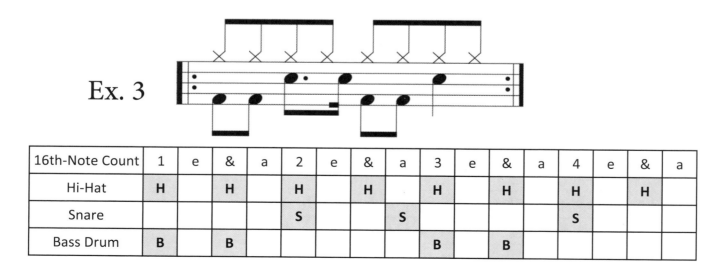

Ex. 3

16th-Note Count	1	e	&	a	2	e	&	a	3	e	&	a	4	e	&	a
Hi-Hat	H		H		H		H		H		H		H		H	
Snare					S			S					S			
Bass Drum	B		B						B		B					

Ex. 4

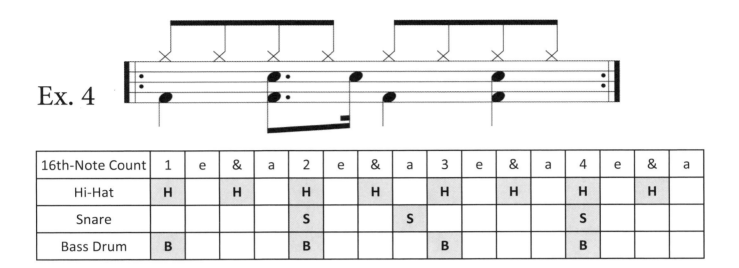

16th-Note Count	1	e	&	a	2	e	&	a	3	e	&	a	4	e	&	a
Hi-Hat	H		H		H		H		H		H		H		H	
Snare					S		S						S			
Bass Drum	B				B				B				B			

Ex. 5

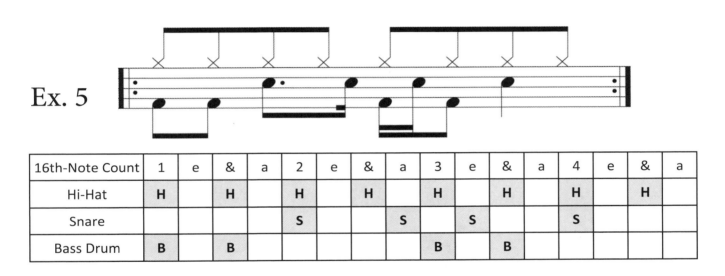

16th-Note Count	1	e	&	a	2	e	&	a	3	e	&	a	4	e	&	a
Hi-Hat	H		H		H		H		H		H		H		H	
Snare					S		S		S				S			
Bass Drum	B		B						B		B					

Now let's try playing those same beats with quarter notes on the hi-hat.

Ex. 1

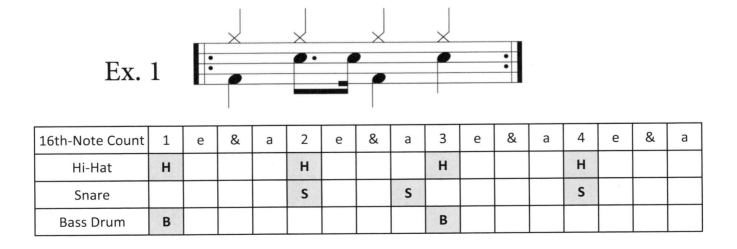

16th-Note Count	1	e	&	a	2	e	&	a	3	e	&	a	4	e	&	a
Hi-Hat	H				H				H				H			
Snare					S				S				S			
Bass Drum	B								B							

Ex. 2

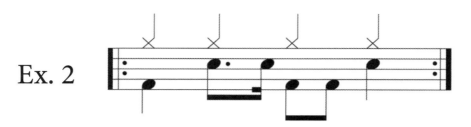

16th-Note Count	1	e	&	a	2	e	&	a	3	e	&	a	4	e	&	a
Hi-Hat	H				H				H				H			
Snare						S				S			S			
Bass Drum	B										B	B				

Ex. 3

16th-Note Count	1	e	&	a	2	e	&	a	3	e	&	a	4	e	&	a
Hi-Hat	H				H				H				H			
Snare						S				S			S			
Bass Drum	B		B						B		B					

Ex. 4

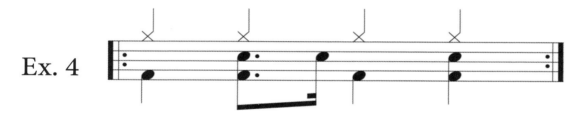

16th-Note Count	1	e	&	a	2	e	&	a	3	e	&	a	4	e	&	a
Hi-Hat	H				H				H				H			
Snare						S				S			S			
Bass Drum	B				B				B				B			

Ex. 5

16th-Note Count	1	e	&	a	2	e	&	a	3	e	&	a	4	e	&	a
Hi-Hat	H				H				H				H			
Snare						S				S	S		S			
Bass Drum	B		B						B		B					

Here are some drum fills that use a flow of constant 16th notes phrased around the snare and toms.

Ex. 1

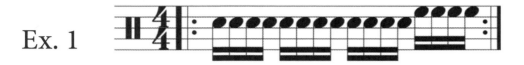

16th-Note Count	1	e	&	a	2	e	&	a	3	e	&	a	4	e	&	a
Tom 1													T1	T1	T1	T1
Snare	S	S	S	S	S	S	S	S	S	S	S	S				

Ex. 2

16th-Note Count	1	e	&	a	2	e	&	a	3	e	&	a	4	e	&	a
Snare	S	S	S	S	S	S	S	S	S	S	S	S				
Tom 2													T2	T2	T2	T2

Ex. 3

16th-Note Count	1	e	&	a	2	e	&	a	3	e	&	a	4	e	&	a
Tom 1					T1	T1	T1	T1								
Snare	S	S	S	S					S	S	S	S				
Tom 2													T2	T2	T2	T2

Ex. 4

16th-Note Count	1	e	&	a	2	e	&	a	3	e	&	a	4	e	&	a
Tom 1																
Snare	S	S	S	S					S	S	S	S				
Tom 2					T2	T2	T2	T2					T2	T2	T2	T2

Ex. 5

16th-Note Count	1	e	&	a	2	e	&	a	3	e	&	a	4	e	&	a
Tom 1									T1	T1	T1	T1				
Snare	S	S	S	S	S	S	S	S								
Tom 2													T2	T2	T2	T2

Ex. 6

16th-Note Count	1	e	&	a	2	e	&	a	3	e	&	a	4	e	&	a
Tom 1					T1	T1	T1	T1			T1	T1				
Snare	S	S	S	S					S	S			S	S		
Tom 2															T2	T2

Now let's try to play our previous fills after one measure of a favorite groove.
Here is a fun option.

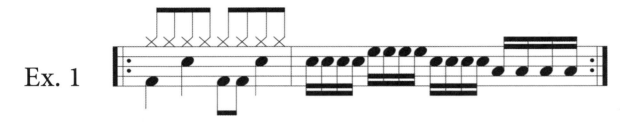

Ex. 1

16th-Note Count	1	e	&	a	2	e	&	a	3	e	&	a	4	e	&	a
Hi-Hat	H		H		H		H		H		H		H		H	
Tom 1																
Snare					S								S			
Tom 2																
Bass Drum	B								B		B					

16th-Note Count	1	e	&	a	2	e	&	a	3	e	&	a	4	e	&	a
Hi-Hat																
Tom 1					T1	T1	T1	T1								
Snare	S	S	S	S					S	S	S	S				
Tom 2													T2	T2	T2	T2
Bass Drum																

It's more common to play drum fills at the end of four-measure phrases. Try practicing the previous exercises again, but repeat your favorite fun groove three times before playing the fill.

PEA SOUP: MMM-MMM GOOD!

"Pea soup" is a phrase used by some drummers to describe the sound that results from playing the hi-hat with a lot of attitude in order to add "flavor" to the beat. Pea soup can be achieved in a variety of ways. Some drummers get the result by playing an open hi-hat sound followed by a quick closed hi-hat sound. They may also strike the hi-hat cymbals with attitude and focus on accenting the open sound to make the hi-hat **bark**. This can create different sonic **colors**. It's very common for drummers to get a variety of sounds out of the same drum or cymbal by simply striking it differently. You can use the pea-soup approach to create two different hi-hat colors, by playing the open sound with the shank of the drumstick and the closed sound with the tip. You can also play the open sound on the edge of the cymbals or strike the top cymbal closer to the bell (center). While the concept of pea soup is simple, the level of difficulty can increase depending on how much flavor you want to add to your beats. The most important thing to remember is not to overdo it. A drummer must always maintain good time and meter. Too much extra flavor can interfere with the beat. Just like cooking a favorite recipe, you must use the right amount of each ingredient. Practice with a metronome, and find the right balance.

Here's an exercise that focuses on the hi-hat by itself to help master the pea-soup sound. The open sound is indicated with an "o" over the note.

Now apply that sound (open hi-hat on the "&" of 4) to some of the grooves you learned in earlier chapters.

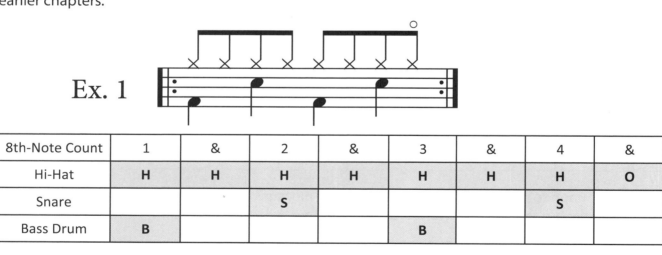

Ex. 1

8th-Note Count	1	&	2	&	3	&	4	&
Hi-Hat	H	H	H	H	H	H	H	O
Snare			S				S	
Bass Drum	B				B			

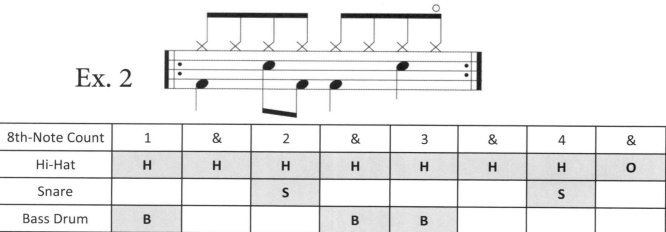

Ex. 2

8th-Note Count	1	&	2	&	3	&	4	&
Hi-Hat	H	H	H	H	H	H	H	O
Snare			S				S	
Bass Drum	B			B	B			

Ex. 3

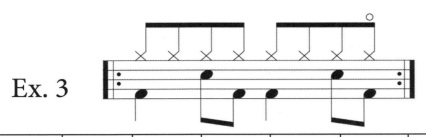

8th-Note Count	1	&	2	&	3	&	4	&
Hi-Hat	H	H	H	H	H	H	H	O
Snare			S				S	
Bass Drum	B			B	B			B

Ex. 4

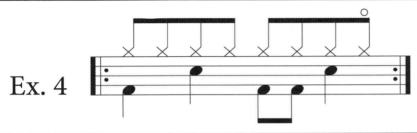

8th-Note Count	1	&	2	&	3	&	4	&
Hi-Hat	H	H	H	H	H	H	H	O
Snare			S				S	
Bass Drum	B				B	B		

Ex. 5

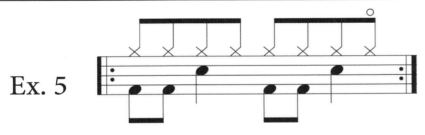

8th-Note Count	1	&	2	&	3	&	4	&
Hi-Hat	H	H	H	H	H	H	H	O
Snare			S				S	
Bass Drum	B	B			B	B		

Ex. 6

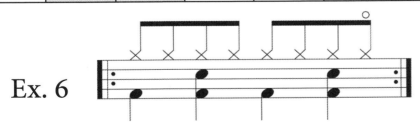

8th-Note Count	1	&	2	&	3	&	4	&
Hi-Hat	H	H	H	H	H	H	H	O
Snare			S				S	
Bass Drum	B		B		B		B	

Now move the open hi-hat sound to the "&" of beat 3.

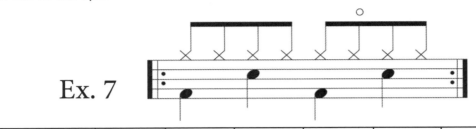

Ex. 7

8th-Note Count	1	&	2	&	3	&	4	&
Hi-Hat	H	H	H	H	H	O	H	H
Snare			S				S	
Bass Drum	B				B			

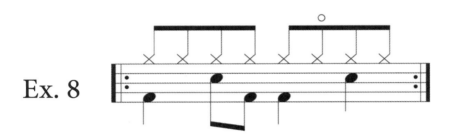

Ex. 8

8th-Note Count	1	&	2	&	3	&	4	&
Hi-Hat	H	H	H	H	H	O	H	H
Snare			S				S	
Bass Drum	B			B	B			

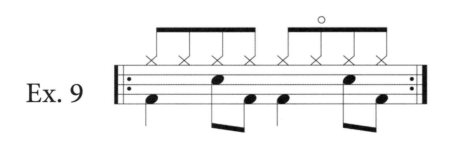

Ex. 9

8th-Note Count	1	&	2	&	3	&	4	&
Hi-Hat	H	H	H	H	H	O	H	H
Snare			S				S	
Bass Drum	B			B	B			B

Ex. 10

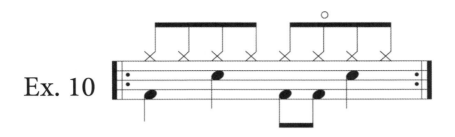

8th-Note Count	1	&	2	&	3	&	4	&
Hi-Hat	H	H	H	H	H	O	H	H
Snare			S				S	
Bass Drum	B				B	B		

Ex. 11

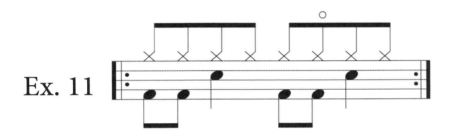

8th-Note Count	1	&	2	&	3	&	4	&
Hi-Hat	H	H	H	H	H	O	H	H
Snare			S				S	
Bass Drum	B	B			B	B		

Ex. 12

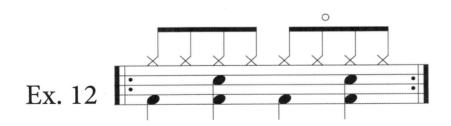

8th-Note Count	1	&	2	&	3	&	4	&
Hi-Hat	H	H	H	H	H	O	H	H
Snare			S				S	
Bass Drum	B		B		B		B	

Here are the same beats with the open hi-hat now on the "&" of beat 2.

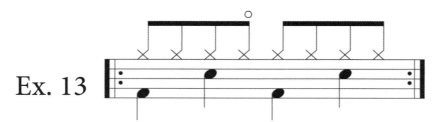

Ex. 13

8th-Note Count	1	&	2	&	3	&	4	&
Hi-Hat	H	H	H	O	H	H	H	H
Snare			S				S	
Bass Drum	B				B			

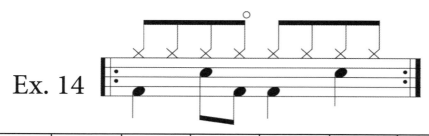

Ex. 14

8th-Note Count	1	&	2	&	3	&	4	&
Hi-Hat	H	H	H	O	H	H	H	H
Snare			S				S	
Bass Drum	B			B	B			

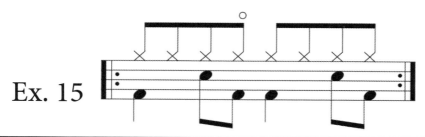

Ex. 15

8th-Note Count	1	&	2	&	3	&	4	&
Hi-Hat	H	H	H	O	H	H	H	H
Snare			S				S	
Bass Drum	B			B	B			B

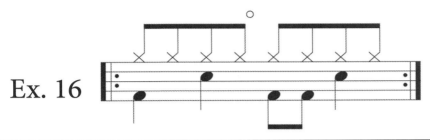

Ex. 16

8th-Note Count	1	&	2	&	3	&	4	&
Hi-Hat	H	H	H	O	H	H	H	H
Snare			S				S	
Bass Drum	B				B	B		

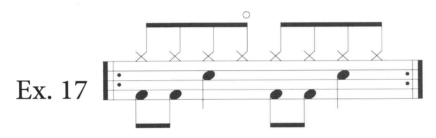

Ex. 17

8th-Note Count	1	&	2	&	3	&	4	&
Hi-Hat	H	H	H	O	H	H	H	H
Snare			S				S	
Bass Drum	B	B			B	B		

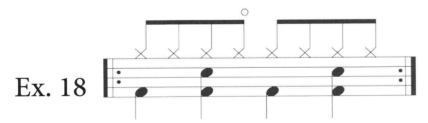

Ex. 18

8th-Note Count	1	&	2	&	3	&	4	&
Hi-Hat	H	H	H	O	H	H	H	H
Snare			S				S	
Bass Drum	B		B		B		B	

Now you're cookin'. Soup's on!

All drummers should come up with their own recipe for "pea soup" by making it their own. Experiment by playing with different attitudes and colors in order to come up with a flavor that works for you. Remember: You're the chef!

GOING GLOBAL: WORLD BEATS

Drums create a universal language of rhythm. Each country and culture has its own version of popular percussion music. Here are a few of the most recognized beats.

Tour the world without ever leaving your drumset.

Music is a universal language that can be shared by all people, even if they don't speak the same dialect. Use these beats as a jumping-off point to explore the music and rhythms of other countries from around the globe.

Motown: This is a style of soul music with a distinct pop influence. Motown drummers introduced a variety of distinctive drum fills that are often imitated today.

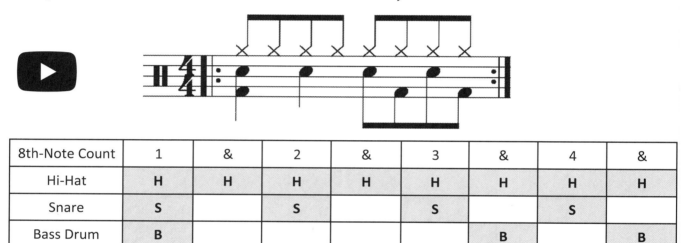

8th-Note Count	1	&	2	&	3	&	4	&
Hi-Hat	H	H	H	H	H	H	H	H
Snare	S		S		S		S	
Bass Drum	B					B		B

Latin: This encompasses a wide range of dance music that incorporates Latin-American rhythms, including cha-cha, mambo, meringue, and samba.

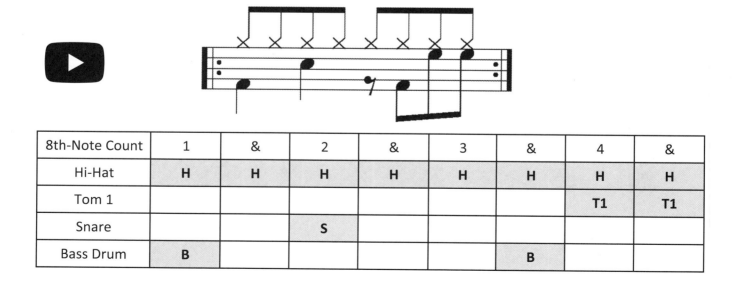

8th-Note Count	1	&	2	&	3	&	4	&
Hi-Hat	H	H	H	H	H	H	H	H
Tom 1							T1	T1
Snare			S					
Bass Drum	B					B		

Disco: A popular style of dance music from the 1970s, disco relied heavily on repetitive bass rhythms and solid four-on-the-floor drumming.

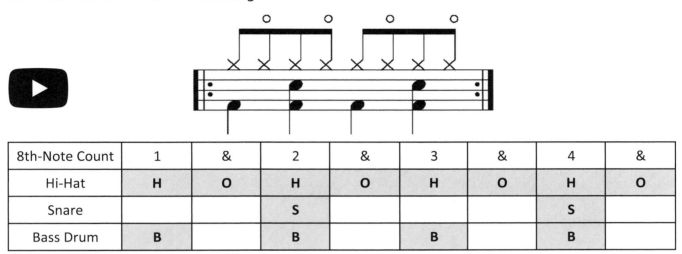

8th-Note Count	1	&	2	&	3	&	4	&
Hi-Hat	H	O	H	O	H	O	H	O
Snare			S				S	
Bass Drum	B		B		B		B	

Country: This American western music often features a distinctive beat that resembles the sound of a train. It's played with consecutive notes on the snare, with accents on the upbeats.

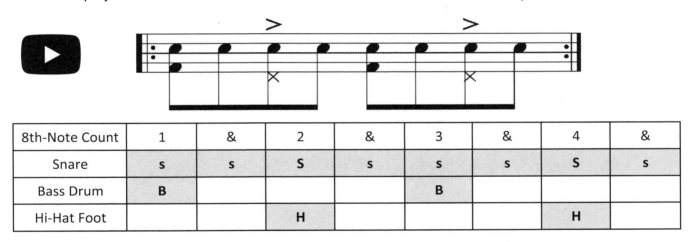

8th-Note Count	1	&	2	&	3	&	4	&
Snare	s	s	S	s	s	s	S	s
Bass Drum	B				B			
Hi-Hat Foot			H				H	

Calypso: A Caribbean style of music that includes a syncopated style of drumming.

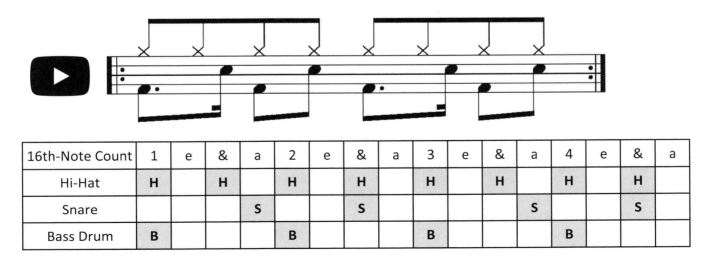

16th-Note Count	1	e	&	a	2	e	&	a	3	e	&	a	4	e	&	a
Hi-Hat	H		H		H		H		H		H		H		H	
Snare			S		S						S				S	
Bass Drum	B				B				B				B			

YOUR FIRST DRUM SOLO!
Always a crowd pleaser, the drum solo is the time to show off your chops!

Although no one knows for sure who played the first drum solo, we do know that early big band and swing drummers were among the first to integrate them into performances. As music evolved, so did the drum solo. Drummers later came up with all kinds of gimmicks to make their solos more exciting, including turning their drumsets upside-down and flying above the crowd.

Some famous songs that incorporate drum solos include:

"Sing, Sing, Sing" (Gene Krupa, Benny Goodman Orchestra)
"Not So Quiet Please" (Buddy Rich, Tommy Dorsey Orchestra)
"Caravan" (Jo Jones, Coleman Hawkins Quintet)
"Moby Dick" (John Bonham, Led Zeppelin)
"Toad" (Ginger Baker, Cream)
"The Mule" (Ian Paice, Deep Purple)
"Wipeout" (Ron Wilson, the Surfaris)
"In-a-Gadda-Da-Vida" (Ron Bushy, Iron Butterfly)
"YYZ" (Neil Peart, Rush)
"Frankenstein" (Chuck Ruff, Edgar Winter Group)
"Take Five" (Joe Morello, Dave Brubeck Quartet)
"Soul Sacrifice" (Michael Shrieve, Santana)

Here's a thirteen-measure drum solo to practice that combines many of the things we've covered in the book. By this point, you should be familiar enough with music notation to get through the solo without the *FUNdamentals* notation tables. If you need a refresher, refer back to the various sections in the book where we covered the "Money Beats," "Pea Soup," and drum fills. We've also posted the tables for this solo at moderndrummer.com/fundamentalsofdrumming if you would like to download them. Have Fun!

TIPS AND TRICKS

Here are some final tips for improving the skills we've developed so far.

Find Your Groove

The groove is the heart and soul of a song. In most cases, it is controlled by the backbeat and creates the emotional rhythm that gives feeling to music. Some of the best drummers throughout the history of music were able to master the groove and play their drums in a way that expresses feelings. Take time to find your own unique way of playing.

Respect the Quarter Note

The quarter note is often referred to as "the king," as it is the most prominent note in popular music. Remember to always respect the quarter note! You'll be spending a lot of time together.

Make It a Combo

Combining snare and bass drum patterns is a great way to build foot strength. Play one 4/4 bar of 8th-note single strokes (R-L-R-L-R-L-R-L) with the hands, followed by a second bar of 8th-note single strokes with the feet. Repeat this pattern, alternating between hands and feet, until the foot muscles become loose and relaxed.

Working the Weaker Hand

Everyone has a dominant hand, whether he or she is right- or left-handed. Drummers need to use both hands, so it's a good idea to try playing the patterns and exercises in this book while leading with the less-dominant hand. Try playing the hi-hat using an open-hand technique with the left hand on the hi-hat and the right hand on the snare (vice versa for left-handed players). This helps develop equal strength between the hands.

Get Marching

Many American-based patriotic songs are written in marching time, including "You're a Grand Old Flag." Music teachers like to compare quarter-note time values to a walking tempo, while comparing 8th-note time values to a running pace. Try playing on a pad or snare in a standing position while marching in time. This helps develop a sense of rhythm, as your hands and feet are all moving to the beat.

Endurance

Another big part of being a drummer is having endurance. That means you can play the drums for some time without getting tired. Faster subdivisions, like 16th notes, can be quite a workout. Start slowly. Play them at a comfortable tempo, and then increase the speed over time. Just like in sports, it takes practice and exercise to get good at drumming!

FUN AND GAMES

Sometimes children will not have the patience or desire to practice. One day they may bang away endlessly, while the next day they show zero interest in the drums. This is completely normal and should be anticipated, especially with younger children. Even adult musicians can lack the motivation to practice their instrument from time to time.

It is up to the adult to decide whether or not to persuade the child who obviously doesn't want to play. This requires caution, as the wrong response may ultimately push him or her away from further learning. We recommend using these moments as an opportunity to step away from the standard exercises and simply have some fun. Sometimes the best way to get a child's attention (and keep it) is to take familiar classroom games and translate them to the drumset. Here are some suggestions.

Simon Says: This is one of the first games taught at the preschool level and should be familiar to most elementary school students. It provides an opportunity for the child to bang away while reinforcing the parts of the drumset. Say, "Simon says, hit the snare drum two times," or "Simon says, hit the ride cymbal once." Work your way around the drumkit, and mix it up. You can also play a variation of this with older children by incorporating the rudiments and saying, "Simon says, play a single-stroke roll." Or add the feet, saying, "Simon says, open and close the hi-hat." The goal of this game is to grab their attention as they anticipate.

Play It Again, Sam: Often, when children are learning a pattern on the drums, such as a new beat, they have a tendency to work on it until they can play it correctly a single time, and then they stop. The truth is that in order to learn any pattern, it should be repeated over and over to induce mental and muscle memory. In order to motivate children to do this, you can play a game where you count how many times in a row they can play the pattern that's being worked on, and then repeat the game, trying to break the high score.

Copycat: This game requires that both the adult and child have sticks. It is most effectively played on a single practice pad. The adult and child should sit facing one another with the pad between them. First, the adult plays a pattern, or some simple strokes, and then the child tries to match it. Start out with simple strokes, and remind the child to maintain proper grip and a consistent stick height. As you progress, add some dynamics, tapping with hard and soft strokes. After a while, switch roles and ask the child to compose some beats for you to match.

Syllable Songs: Drumming in sync with the words to a familiar song can be a fun way to play with rhythm. Popular songs like "London Bridge" work well, with the child striking a beat with each syllable of the verse: "Lon-don Bridge is fall-ing down…"

Cadences

Everyone loves a parade, and marching bands have been stepping out to the beat of drummers for hundreds of years. Drum lines provide the marching time for the rest of the band and are usually made up of a group of musicians who play snare drums, bass drums, toms, and cymbals. When they are not playing along with the band, drum lines play **cadences** by themselves.

Cadences are special drum-only songs that keep everyone in step. They can be groovy and are sometimes very complex. Here are a few kids' cadences that can be played on a pad or snare drum. The key is to play along with each syllable of the song. Ask the child to say the words aloud as he or she makes each stroke. You may wish to place the pad on a chair or raise the snare stand so the child can stand up and play, and perhaps march in place. Start out slow, and then gradually increase the tempo.

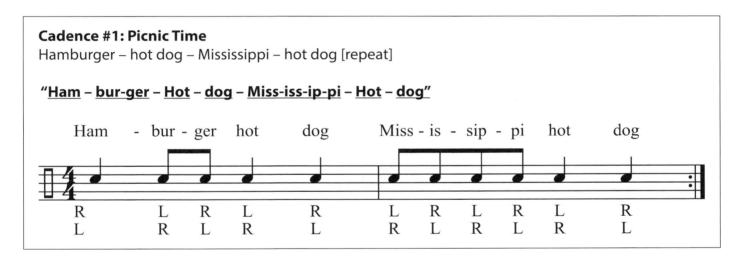

Cadence #1: Picnic Time
Hamburger – hot dog – Mississippi – hot dog [repeat]

"Ham – bur-ger – Hot – dog – Miss-iss-ip-pi – Hot – dog"

Cadence #2: The Name Game
Use your name to create a cadence.

"My name is [insert name here]."

PARTING PHILOSOPHY

Simply put, drums are my passion. I love drums, and playing them is all I have ever wanted to do. Drums have taken me around the world and helped to introduce me to new places, faces, cultures, and food. (Yum!) Always remember that you can do whatever you set your mind to. Never give up. If you want to get good at playing the drums, just practice. Some say practice makes perfect, but nobody is perfect. Practice simply makes you the best you can be, and that in itself is a perfect concept. Work on things that you can't do, and make little improvements every day. It's better to practice twenty minutes a day than ten hours once a week. Repetition and practice is the key to getting good, but remember to keep it fun. I sure hope you enjoyed our time together here. Be sure to be part of our active online community, and let us know how your drumming is coming along. We can't wait to see what you can do!

High fives and hugs! —Rich

Rich's favorite drummers to check out: Gene Krupa (Benny Goodman), Liberty DeVitto (Billy Joel), John Bonham (Led Zeppelin), Stewart Copeland (the Police), and Carmine Appice (Vanilla Fudge).

This entire workbook has been designed to provide you with all kinds of fun exercises and activities, and we hope you've enjoyed them. If you do develop an interest in learning more about the drums, we highly recommend you take drum lessons with a percussion teacher and get involved in your school's music program. Rich and I are products of public school music programs, and we had a lot of fun while playing in school concerts, band festivals, and parades. We still talk to our teachers today, as they had a lasting, positive influence on our lives. Playing the drums changed my life, and I am very thankful that I can now share my passion with my own children and with you. Even as a grown-up, I am still learning and improving. Never stop learning, and never stop having fun while you do it.

Keep that beat! —Michael

Michael's favorite drummers to check out: Jo Jones (Count Basie), Phil Rudd (AC/DC), Chris Dave (the Drumhedz), Jon Farriss (INXS), and Alan Myers (Devo).

Pictured, from top: Rich with his first snare drum and marching at Texas Tech University, and Michael at his first gig at thirteen and as drum line co-captain.